THE SOVIET PARLIAMENT

(A REFERENCE BOOK)

PROGRESS PUBLISHERS • MOSCOW

1967

Translated from the Russian

Edited by M. Saifulin

Contributed by V. Grigoryev, F. Kalinychev, V. Kirin,
Y. Korolyov, I. Krivenko, R. Kulik, A. Levitsky, A. Lu-
kyanov, N. Nikolayeva, V. Rakushin, M. Revsky,
P. Sedugin, B. Tokmakov, G. Vasilyev, V. Vasilyev,
V. Yevgenyev and B. Zhaleiko
Russian text edited by F. Kalinychev and V. Vasilyev

СОВЕТСКИЙ ПАРЛАМЕНТ

На английском языке

First printing 1967

Printed in the Union of Soviet Socialist Republics

CONTENTS

INTRODUCTION

The Union of Soviet Socialist Republics is the first state in history where no class enjoys special privileges and where the exploitation of man by man has been abolished. The Soviet state came into existence in 1917, following the triumph of the October Revolution in Russia which overthrew the reactionary bourgeois-landowner system and transferred power to the Soviets. The workers, peasants and intellectuals are the masters of their country, for all the social wealth and all political power belong to them.

Territorially—22,400,000 square kilometres—the Soviet Union is the largest country in the world. On January 1, 1967, it had a population of 234 million as against 159,200,000 in 1913. An indicative trend is the growth of the urban population: in 1913 the ratio between the urban and rural population was 18 and 82 per cent; in 1940—33 and 67; in 1959—48 and 52; and in 1966—54 and 46 per cent. The class structure of the population has changed beyond recognition. There are only two classes at present—the working class and the peasantry—and a social stratum of working intellectuals. In 1965, the factory, office and professional workers comprised 75.4 per cent, and the peasants 24.6 per cent of the population.

There has been a particularly marked increase of brain workers. In 1926 they numbered a mere 2,600,000 and early in 1966—26 million. This is an important result of the socialist transformations in the country and of the cultural revolution.

In Soviet years the U.S.S.R. has become a major world power. In 1913 tsarist Russia accounted for a little over 4 per cent of the world industrial product. In 1966 the Soviet Union contributed 20 per cent to the world industrial product. For the output of many industrial and agricultural items the Soviet Union holds first place in the world. It also occupies a leading position in world science.

The U.S.S.R. is a federal state, consisting of 15 Union Republics, namely:

Russian Soviet Federative Socialist Republic,
Ukrainian Soviet Socialist Republic,
Byelorussian Soviet Socialist Republic,

Uzbek Soviet Socialist Republic,
Kazakh Soviet Socialist Republic,
Georgian Soviet Socialist Republic,
Azerbaijan Soviet Socialist Republic,
Lithuanian Soviet Socialist Republic,
Moldavian Soviet Socialist Republic,
Latvian Soviet Socialist Republic,
Kirghiz Soviet Socialist Republic,
Tajik Soviet Socialist Republic,
Armenian Soviet Socialist Republic,
Turkmen Soviet Socialist Republic,
Estonian Soviet Socialist Republic.

In addition there are 20 Autonomous Republics, eight Autonomous Regions and 10 National Areas which are incorporated in some of the Union Republics.

The Soviet state has a multinational population. The constantly developing forms of the statehood of the Soviet nations and nationalities, based as they are on socialist principles, are embodied in the entire system of Soviets, including the Supreme Soviet of the U.S.S.R. This is one of the greatest achievements of the Soviet Union, one of the vast advantages of the popular rule consolidated in the form of the Soviets of Working People's Deputies, which are the instrument of the people's social, political and national liberation and development.

SUPREME SOVIET OF THE U.S.S.R.—HIGHEST
ORGAN OF STATE POWER

The Supreme Soviet of the U.S.S.R. is the highest representative body of the Soviet people.

In 1967 the Soviet peoples celebrate the 50th anniversary of the October Socialist Revolution and the Soviet state. The all-embracing system of representative bodies of a new type—the Soviets of Working People's Deputies—was set up and tested by practice, by the rich experience of socialist and communist construction. Therein lies one of the major achievements of the Soviet state.

The working people actively participate in the solution of all political, economic, social and cultural problems through their representative organs.

The uniform system of Soviets crowned by the Supreme Soviet of the U.S.S.R. is made up of the Supreme Soviets of the 15 Union Republics, the Supreme Soviets of the 20 Autonomous Republics, 111 Regional and Territory Soviets, Regional Soviets of the eight Autonomous Regions, Area Soviets of the 10 National Areas, over 2,500 District Soviets and over 45,000 Village, Township, Town and Ward (in big cities) Soviets of Working People's Deputies.

The Soviet deputies (of whom there are over 2,000,000) are aided by more than 23 million activists. This is a convincing indication of the consistent application of Lenin's dictum that "it is the people united by the Soviets who must govern the state".

The Soviets of Workers' and Peasants' Deputies came into being during the Russian revolution of 1905-07 as organs of the popular insurrection. They were the embryo of the new revolutionary power of the people. The Soviets reappeared in February 1917 when the tsarist autocracy was overthrown. However, all political power was transferred into the hands of the Soviets only on October 25 (November 7), 1917, after the armed uprising triumphed in Petrograd. This victory of the workers and peasants in the socialist revolution was legally embodied in the decrees of the Soviet Government. The first decrees—Decree on Land and Decree on Peace—were adopted by the 2nd Congress of Soviets on October 25. Of great historical importance was the Declaration of the Rights of the Toiling and Exploited People approved by the 3rd All-Russia Congress of Soviets in January 1918.

The establishment of the Soviets, organs of popular rule, gave the people the real possibility of administering political, economic and social affairs. Soviet society gave birth to socialist democracy, which is the broadest, most representative and just democracy known to man.

Socialism implies that all material and spiritual wealth is transferred into the hands of the working people, that the state is administered by them. It also implies that the masses, liberated from exploitation, decide all social matters either themselves or through their representatives.

The system of representation which comes into existence with the victory of a socialist revolution and undergoes constant improvement, guarantees that the people have a real say on all crucial problems of social development. The people have a vested interest in the maximum possible representation of all social groups, of all strata of the working people in the organs of power. For only in this way can an organ of power express the will and aspirations of the people and decide the most intricate problems with an eye to all their specific interests.

Therefore, the keynote of all representative systems of the socialist type, including the Soviets, is *the broadest possible representation of all the people in these bodies*. They represent all the classes of socialist society, all its social strata, all nations and nationalities, and all trades and professions.

Another important feature of a socialist representative system is that the organs of power are *working corporations vested with authority both to decide matters and implement the adopted decisions, i.e., to pass legislation and to administer*.

The people of the socialist countries participate in the administration of all important government and social affairs through their authorised representatives in the higher legislative bodies. The activities of the deputies are organised in such a way as to make them accessible and understandable to the masses, to link them closely with productive labour and secure a swift, economical and proper solution of problems and the translation of the appropriate measures into life.

These features underlie the structure and activities of the Soviet state, which was founded under the guidance of Lenin. They are reflected in the system of organs of state power both on an all-Union and republican scale, in the organisation of these organs on various levels. The Congresses of Soviets, the Central Executive Committees (CEC), the CEC Presidiums of the U.S.S.R. and of its constituent Republics, their auxiliary and executive bodies made up a system of the higher representative bodies of the state, which fitted in with the requirements of Soviet society in the 1920s and in the early 1930s. This system was first legislatively embodied in the 1924 Constitution of the U.S.S.R. and subsequently in the 1936 Constitution of the U.S.S.R., as well as in the Constitutions of the Union and Autonomous Republics.

In 1922 the independent Soviet Republics united in a single federal state—the Union of Soviet Socialist Republics—by voluntary and unanimous agreement. Since then this federal state has expanded.

Today it has 15 members, each of which has equal rights that stem from its sovereignty, and not a single one of them has privileges or exclusive rights vis-à-vis any other Soviet Republic. The Soviet Federation provides a striking example of firm co-operation and fraternal mutual assistance between all the nations and nationalities inhabiting the country.

The federal structure of the U.S.S.R. determines the pattern of its higher organs of state power and the volume of their jurisdiction.

In conformity with the federal Constitution (Art. 30) the highest organ of state power is the Supreme Soviet of the U.S.S.R. It is vested with the plentitude of state power and expresses the sovereignty of all the Soviet peoples. It exercises all rights vested in the Union of Soviet Socialist Republics insofar as they do not, by virtue of the 1936 Constitution, come within the jurisdiction of other organs that are accountable to the Supreme Soviet of the U.S.S.R., i.e., the Presidium of the Supreme Soviet, the Council of Ministers and the ministries of the U.S.S.R.

The Supreme Soviet of the U.S.S.R. is a truly popular parliament. It is formed to act as the highest representative organ of the entire Soviet people. It is elected for a term of four years by the citizens of the country on the basis of universal, equal and direct suffrage by secret ballot. As soon as its term of office expires, the Presidium of the Supreme Soviet of the U.S.S.R. appoints new elections not later than two months after the date of the expiry of its term. The Supreme Soviet is a broad collegium of the popular representatives who are called upon to express the will of the people and reflect their best interests. Every member of the Supreme Soviet is entitled to participate in the discussion and adoption of bills, to put the laws into practice and to control the activities of state administrative bodies.

As the highest organ of state power the Supreme Soviet of the U.S.S.R. was formed as a result of the general election held in 1937 in accordance with the 1936 Constitution. Before this Constitution came into force, the higher organs of state power in the country had been the Congress of Soviets of the U.S.S.R., the Central Executive Committee of the U.S.S.R. and the Presidium of the CEC of the U.S.S.R.

This particular system of higher organs of Soviet power was set up immediately following the October Revolution of 1917 and was borrowed by all the Soviet Republics and legislatively embodied in their constitutions (the case in point was the Russian Federation Constitution of 1918). This system was organised in such a way as to take into account the tasks and specific features of the Union state. Thus, there was an obvious continuity in the basic traditions proper to the structure and the activities of the higher organs of power.

The Congress of Soviets of the U.S.S.R. consisted of representatives from towns and townships elected on the basis of one delegate per 25,000 electors and from the rural population—one delegate per

125,000 electors. Delegates to the All-Union Congresses of Soviets were elected at Regional or Territory Congresses of Soviets, the Congresses of Soviets in the Autonomous Republics and the Autonomous Regions, and also at the Congresses of Soviets in the Union Republics which had no regional divisions.

Customarily, congresses were convened once a year, and beginning with 1927—once in two years.

The All-Union Congresses debated the most important political, economic, social and cultural problems and international affairs.

The exclusive jurisdiction of the U.S.S.R. Congress of Soviets covered the approval and modification of the basic principles of the U.S.S.R. Constitution, the elaboration of the principles of the state budget and national economic planning, the establishment of the general principles of current legislation and also the guidance of all state organs and control over their activities.

Since 1922, the year the U.S.S.R. was formed, there have been seven regular U.S.S.R. Congresses of Soviets and one extraordinary congress (the 8th, in 1936).

The representation quota in the Congresses increased steadily. In the election to the 2nd All-Russia Congress of Soviets a total of 673 delegates were elected, whereas the number of delegates to the 10th All-Russia Congress rose to 2,215. Between the 1st and 8th All-Union Congresses the number of delegates with powers to decide increased from 1,673 to 2,016. Moreover, 70 to 80 per cent of the delegates were, as a rule, workers or peasants.

In the interim between the Congresses, the highest state organ of the U.S.S.R. was the Central Executive Committee of the U.S.S.R., which consisted of two chambers, the Soviet of the Union and the Soviet of Nationalities. The Soviet of the Union was elected by the All-Union Congress of Soviets from representatives of the Union Republics in proportion to the population of each Republic. The Soviet of Nationalities was formed on the basis of five representatives from each Union and Autonomous Republic and one representative from each Autonomous Region, all of whom being endorsed by the All-Union Congress. Between 1922 and 1937, the membership of the Central Executive Committee increased from 472 to 757.

Both chambers of the CEC of the U.S.S.R.—the Soviet of the Union and the Soviet of Nationalities—enjoyed equal rights. The CEC functioned in the form of sessions, the ordinary sessions being convened not less than three times in the interim between Congresses.

Legislation and the administration of the country was concentrated in the hands of the CEC of the U.S.S.R., which promulgated codes and decrees, adopted decisions, issued orders, appointed the Soviet Government—the Council of People's Commissars—and, when necessary, changed its composition, and guided and controlled the activities of the other higher state organs.

In the interim between sessions of the CEC of the U.S.S.R., the highest legislative, executive and administrative organ of state power was the Presidium of the CEC of the U.S.S.R. It was a permanent body and was elected by the above-mentioned Committee. It included the Presidents of the CEC of the U.S.S.R. (one from each of the Union Republic) and also the members of the Presidiums of the Soviet of the Union and of the Soviet of Nationalities. One-third of the members of the Presidium were elected at a joint sitting of both chambers.

The concurrent Presidents of the CEC of the U.S.S.R. were M. I. Kalinin (since December 30, 1922), elected from the Russian Federation; G. I. Petrovsky (since December 30, 1922), elected from the Ukrainian Republic; N. N. Narimanov (since December 30, 1922) and G. Musabekov (since May 21, 1925), elected from the Transcaucasian Soviet Federative Socialist Republic; A. G. Chervyakov (since December 30, 1922), elected from the Byelorussian Republic; N. Aitakov (since May 21, 1925), elected from the Turkmen Republic; F. Khodzhayev (since May 21, 1925), elected from the Uzbek Republic; M. Nasratulla (since March 18, 1931) and A. R. Rakhimbayev (since January 4, 1934), elected from the Tajik Republic.

The Presidium of the CEC watched over the implementation of the Constitution of the U.S.S.R., and of the decisions taken by the Congresses of Soviets and the CEC of the U.S.S.R. It passed decrees, decisions and orders which were binding on all lower state organs.

The Presidium was accountable and subordinate to the CEC of the U.S.S.R.

In the interim between sessions of the CEC, its functions were discharged by the Presidium, whose decisions were subject to final approval by the CEC of the U.S.S.R. The Presidium also had exclusive jurisdiction, which it exercised continuously. All major acts which determined the principles governing political and social life had to be considered and approved solely by an All-Union Congress of Soviets or the Central Executive Committee of the U.S.S.R.

In conformity with Article 78 of the Statute of the Central Executive Committee of the U.S.S.R., the CEC and its Presidium set up commissions to deal with current legislation and administration. In particular, the CEC of each convocation used to form Budgetary Commissions, which duly represented the central organs and those of the Union Republics. Thus, on April 25, 1926, the CEC of the 3rd convocation appointed a Budgetary Commission with a total membership of 96 (15 members from the central bodies, 47 members from the Russian Federation, 16 members from the Ukraine, six members from the Transcaucasian Federative Republic, four members from the Byelorussian Republic, five members from the Uzbek Republic and three members from the Turkmen Republic).

The CEC set up other standing and temporary commissions and committees. They included the Commission for Soviet Building and Organisational Matters, the Commission for the Adjudication of Court

HIGHER ORGANS OF STATE POWER AND ADMINISTRATION UNDER THE 1924 CONSTITUTION OF THE U.S.S.R.

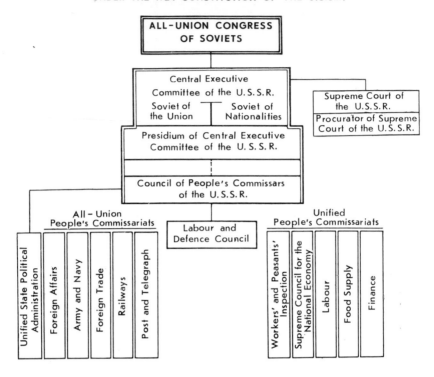

Cases, the Commission for the Examination of Recommendations for the Award of Orders, the Commission for the Consideration of Decisions Taken by Plenary Meetings of the U.S.S.R. Supreme Court, the Central Resettlement Committee, and so forth.

With the victory of socialism in the country the system of its higher organs of power and the procedure of their formation underwent essential changes. The 1936 Constitution abolished the disparities in the electoral law whoch operated in respect of the members of the former exploiting classes and introduced universal, equal and direct suffrage by secret ballot and according to constituencies at all levels—from the rural and town Soviets to the Supreme Soviet of the U.S.S.R.

The three-tier system of state organs—the All-Union Congress of Soviets, the Central Executive Committee of the U.S.S.R. and its Presidium—was replaced by a two-tier system: the Supreme Soviet of the U.S.S.R. and its Presidium. The highest executive and administrative organ of state power is now the Council of Ministers, which handles the current administration of the country.

Thus, the evolution of the Soviet state witnessed big changes in the forms and functions of its organs, in the interrelation between the higher organs of state power and the higher organs of state administration.

The Supreme Soviet of the U.S.S.R. consists of two chambers enjoying equal rights—the Soviet of the Union and the Soviet of Nationalities (Arts. 33 and 37 of the Constitution of the U.S.S.R.).

The idea for a bicameral structure of the Supreme Soviet was advanced and substantiated in Communist Party decisions. The Resolution of the 12th Party Congress in 1923 on the national question emphasised the need to set up, within the system of the higher organs of the U.S.S.R., a special organ representing all the national Republics and national regions on an equal basis.

The present two-chamber system of the highest body enables the Supreme Soviet to heed to the needs of the Soviet peoples, to render them timely assistance, and promote mutual understanding, trust and fraternal co-operation among all the socialist nations.

The Soviet of the Union and the Soviet of Nationalities have equal power to initiate legislation. Sessions of these two chambers begin and terminate simultaneously. Both chambers may consider questions at joint or separate sittings. A law is considered adopted if it is passed by both chambers by a simple majority vote in each. Article 47 of the Constitution of the U.S.S.R. says: in the event of disagreement between the Soviet of the Union and the Soviet of Nationalities, the question is referred for settlement to a conciliation commission formed by the chambers on a parity basis. If the conciliation commission fails to arrive at an agreement or if its decision fails to satisfy one of the chambers, the question is considered for a second time by the chambers. Failing agreement between the two chambers, the Presidium of the Supreme Soviet of the U.S.S.R. dissolves the Supreme Soviet and appoints new elections. In short, neither of the chambers has special privileges or restrictions with regard to the other. Decisions taken by both chambers have equal force. Moreover, the constitutional procedure of settling disagreements is ample proof of the equal status of the chambers and a firm guarantee of their equality.

The truly democratic structure of the Supreme Soviet ensures the consistent implementation of the Communist Party's nationalities policy. As regards its national composition the Supreme Soviet of the U.S.S.R. is an assembly of authorised representatives of all the Soviet nations and nationalities, who have joined to form a federal state.

The Supreme Soviet possesses broad jurisdiction. It is the supreme bearer of the Soviet people's sovereignty and the spokesman of their state will and power. The Soviet Parliament exercises full and exclusive paramountcy over all the other organs of power and administration. The Supreme Soviet of the U.S.S.R. alone is entitled to exercise supreme control over the activities of the Government, Supreme Court and Procurator-General of the U.S.S.R.

Its basic jurisdiction covers: approval and amendment of the Constitution of the U.S.S.R., all-Union legislation; formation of the higher state organs of the U.S.S.R.; appointment and dismissal of high officials of the U.S.S.R.; decision of all major issues of the internal and external policy of the U.S.S.R.; approval of economic development plans and the single State Budget of the U.S.S.R.; supreme control over the activities of state organs and officials.

The legislative power of the U.S.S.R. is exercised exclusively by the Supreme Soviet of the U.S.S.R. (Art. 32 of the Constitution of the U.S.S.R.)

The laws passed by the Supreme Soviet of the U.S.S.R. govern the activities of all organs of state, officials and citizens. While generalising the experience accumulated in political, economic, cultural and defence matters, the Supreme Soviet of the U.S.S.R. adopts legislative acts that are called upon to fix, protect and develop the relationships and orders established in Soviet society. All-Union laws are the supreme expression of the sovereign will of the Soviet people and contain the more general norms.

The legislative process consists of the following stages: 1) introduction of a bill; 2) discussion of a bill; 3) approval of a law; 4) promulgation of a law.

Bills are tabled in the Supreme Soviet by organs or persons entitled to initiate legislation, i.e., to introduce in the legislative body proposals to pass new laws or make amendments and additions to the laws in force or to repeal them. These proposals are examined by the legislative body on their merits.

The right to initiate legislation is exercised by both chambers of the Supreme Soviet of the U.S.S.R. and their standing committees, the deputies of the Supreme Soviet, the Presidium of the Supreme Soviet, the Council of Ministers of the U.S.S.R., the Supreme Court of the U.S.S.R., and also by the Union Republics as represented by their higher organs of state power.

An exceedingly important role in underscoring the necessity for drafting and promulgating new laws is played by the Central Committee of the Communist Party of the Soviet Union. Not infrequently appropriate proposals to this effect are also advanced by the central bodies of the mass organisations of the working people—the All-Union Central Council of Trade Unions, the Central Committee of the Young Communist League, and others.

After hearing a report or a co-report on a bill, the Supreme Soviet of the U.S.S.R. proceeds to discuss the bill on its merits. As a rule, a bill is discussed at a separate sitting of the respective chamber and in the presence of representatives from the press and the public. The deputies of the Supreme Soviet of the U.S.S.R., members of the Soviet

Government, representatives of mass organisations, and scientists take part in the debate on the bill.

When the debate is over, the Supreme Soviet hears the concluding speeches by the rapporteurs or co-rapporteurs, considers amendments moved during the debate and then takes the vote.

Laws are voted by a show of hands. The vote is taken by sections or articles of a law or as a whole. A law is passed by both chambers by a simple majority vote in each. Amendments to the Constitution are adopted by a majority of not less than two-thirds of the votes in each of the chambers of the Supreme Soviet of the U.S.S.R. (Art. 146 of the Constitution of the U.S.S.R.). This is explained by the fact that the Constitution is the fundamental law of the state and forms the juridical basis for current legislation.

The Supreme Soviet of the U.S.S.R. also legislates by endorsing the normative decrees issued by the Presidium of the Supreme Soviet of the U.S.S.R. on political, economic, social and cultural matters.

This legislative procedure is conditioned by the fact that the Supreme Soviet of the U.S.S.R.—the supreme representative body of the working people—regularly meets twice a year. In the interim between its sessions social relations are regulated legally by the other higher organ of state power, which is an organic part of the Supreme Soviet itself—the Presidium of the Supreme Soviet of the U.S.S.R. The decrees issued by the Presidium with a view to amending or supplementing current legislation or to changing the composition of the Council of Ministers of the U.S.S.R. are submitted for approval to the Supreme Soviet of the U.S.S.R. at its regular sessions.

The Supreme Soviet of the U.S.S.R. exercises its legislative function by two methods:

1) by discussing, scrutinising and adopting constitutional laws or ordinary laws on current issues of the state;

2) by examining and approving the normative decrees issued by the Presidium of the Supreme Soviet of the U.S.S.R. on various economic, social and cultural matters and also the acts to change the composition of the Soviet Government.

Let us cite data on the number of sessions of the Supreme Soviet of the U.S.S.R. of all convocations and the number of acts it has passed (including the approval of decrees).

First convocation (December 12, 1937-February 10, 1946).* There were 12 sessions, which passed 97 acts and approved 33 decrees.

Second convocation (between February 10, 1946 and March 12, 1950). Altogether there were five sessions, which passed 60 legislative acts, including the approval of 30 decrees.

Third convocation (between March 12, 1950 and March 14, 1951).

---

* Elections to the Supreme Soviet of the U.S.S.R. were not held during the war against nazi Germany (1941-1945), when part of Soviet territory was occupied by the Wehrmacht.

Altogether there were five sessions, which passed 41 legislative acts, including the approval of 15 decrees.

Fourth convocation (between March 14, 1954 and March 16, 1958). Altogether there were nine sessions, which passed 121 legislative acts, including the approval of 70 decrees.

Fifth convocation (between March 16, 1958 and March 18, 1962). Altogether there were seven sessions, which passed 131 legislative acts, including the approval of 59 decrees.

Sixth convocation (between March 18, 1962 and June 12, 1966). Altogether there were seven sessions, which passed 111 legislative acts, including the approval of 60 decrees.

Seventh convocation (elected on June 12, 1966). So far there have been two sessions, which have passed 26 legislative acts, including the approval of 15 decrees.

All in all, the 47 sessions of the Supreme Soviet of the U.S.S.R. (seven convocations) passed 587 legislative acts, including the approval of 280 decrees.

A law passed by the Supreme Soviet of the U.S.S.R. is subject to promulgation and comes into force by strictly regulated procedure. The Soviet legislative process does not provide for a separate stage of the approval of a bill equivalent to the third reading, practised in Western parliaments.

Laws passed by the Supreme Soviet of the U.S.S.R. are published in the languages of all the Union Republics and are countersigned by the President and Secretary of the Presidium of the Supreme Soviet

President Podgorny signs the instruments of ratification of the Treaty of Friendship, Co-operation and Mutual Assistance between the U.S.S.R. and the Mongolian People's Republic at a meeting of the Presidium of the Supreme Soviet of the U.S.S.R. on February 11, 1966

of the U.S.S.R. (Art. 40 of the Constitution of the U.S.S.R.) The promulgation of an all-Union law in the languages of all the Union Republics reflects the principle of full equality of the Soviet nations and nationalities and makes an all-Union law understandable to all people, irrespective of their nationality. The all-Union laws have the same force on the territory of all the Union Republics. In the event of divergence between a law of a Union or Autonomous Republic and a law of the Union, the all-Union law prevails, for the all-Union laws express the interests of all people of the U.S.S.R. (Arts. 19 and 20 of the Constitution of the U.S.S.R.) The priority enjoyed by all-Union legislation over republican legislation is due to the integrity of the Soviet federal state.

The promulgation of laws apart, the jurisdiction of the Supreme Soviet covers admission of new republics into the U.S.S.R., approval of changes in the boundaries between Union Republics, the establishment of general procedure governing the relations of the Union Republics with other states, the formulation of principles guiding the organisation of the military formations of the Union Republics, the reorganisation of Autonomous Republics into Union Republics, and approval of the formation of new Autonomous Republics and Autonomous Regions within Union Republics.

Under the Constitution of the U.S.S.R., the Supreme Soviet of the U.S.S.R., when it deems necessary, completely or partially reorganises state organs. Thus, in March 1946 the First Session of the Second Supreme Soviet of the U.S.S.R. reorganised the Council of People's

Commissars into a Council of Ministers, transforming the People's Commissariats into Ministries and giving the Procurator of the U.S.S.R. the title of the Procurator-General of the U.S.S.R.

In 1958 the Supreme Soviet introduced addenda to the Constitution of the U.S.S.R., according to which every Union Republic is represented in the Presidium of the Supreme Soviet of the U.S.S.R. by its Vice-President, and the chairmen of the Council of Ministers of the Union Republics are included in the Government of the U.S.S.R. as members by virtue of their office.

Taking into account the changes in the country's economy and culture, the Supreme Soviet of the U.S.S.R. reorganises, in appropriate cases, ministries and central departments of the U.S.S.R.: unifies or divides them, forms new ones and transforms all-Union into Union-Republican bodies. When necessary, the Supreme Soviet forms State Committees of the Council of Ministers for particular spheres.

The Sixth Session of the Sixth Supreme Soviet held in October 1965 adopted a law on the reorganisation of industrial management and some organs of state administration. This law provided for the formation of a number of all-Union and Union-Republican ministries and for the reorganisation of the Union-Republican State Committee for Research Co-ordination into an all-Union State Committee of the Council of Ministers of the U.S.S.R. for Science and Technology, and of the all-Union State Building Committee into a Union-Republican State Building Committee of the Council of Ministers of the U.S.S.R., and also envisaged the formation of a Union-Republican State Committee for Material and Technical Supply.

The jurisdiction of the Supreme Soviet of the U.S.S.R. also covers control over the observance of the Constitution of the U.S.S.R. and ensurance of conformity of the Constitutions of the Union Republics with the Constitution of the U.S.S.R. Wherever the Supreme Soviet introduces amendments or addenda into the Constitution of the U.S.S.R., it sees to it that the Supreme Soviets of the Union Republics introduce appropriate amendments or addenda into their respective Constitutions. This is governed by Article 16 of the Constitution of the U.S.S.R. stipulating that each Union Republic has its own Constitution, which takes account of the specific features of the Republic and is drawn up in full conformity with the Constitution of the U.S.S.R.

In addition to the afore-mentioned questions, the Supreme Soviet, being the highest organ of state power, may consider, if necessary, any other question that comes within the competence of the Union. Ordinarily, the Supreme Soviet hears the reports by the Soviet Government at its sessions and controls the activities of the Council of Ministers and the Ministries of the U.S.S.R. through the Presidium of the Supreme Soviet and the standing committees of both chambers, through questions put by deputies to the Government as a whole or to individual ministers and also through its appointment, in case of necessity, of investigating and auditing committees on any matter.

Of great significance is the activity of the Supreme Soviet of the U.S.S.R. aimed at preserving world peace and relaxing international tension. A case in point is the Declaration of the Supreme Soviet of February 9, 1959, which provided for the establishment of direct links between the Supreme Soviet of the U.S.S.R. and the parliaments of other states through exchanges of delegations, speeches in parliaments, and the development of friendly relations and co-operation between parliaments, governments and nations, irrespective of their socio-economic system.

To facilitate inter-parliamentary collaboration, the Supreme Soviet of the U.S.S.R. set up a Parliamentary Group, which in 1955 became a member of the Inter-Parliamentary Union. Soviet parliamentarians play a prominent part in that body.

The Supreme Soviet also establishes the main principles of the internal and foreign policies of the U.S.S.R. and settles questions of war and peace. The policy of the Communist Party of the Soviet Union, which purports to secure lasting peace and strengthen Soviet defences against foreign aggression, underlies the activities of the Soviet state organs. On these questions the Supreme Soviet hears the reports of the Council of Ministers and adopts the appropriate decisions.

Expressing the peaceful aspirations of the Soviet peoples, the members of the Supreme Soviet of the U.S.S.R. approve the Soviet Government's proposals on such crucial international issues as general and complete disarmament, the conclusion of a German peace treaty and the settlement of the West Berlin question on this basis, and of a non-aggression treaty between the NATO and Warsaw Treaty countries.

The supreme organ of the Soviet state emphatically denounces the aggressive actions of international reaction and consistently champions peace and co-operation among all states, regardless of their socio-economic systems.

The Supreme Soviet functions under the guidance of the Central Committee of the C.P.S.U., which is the leading and directing force of Soviet society. The Central Committee of the Party submits to the Supreme Soviet legislative proposals on the most important issues of state, economic, social and cultural development. This was the case, for example, with the draft laws on the reorganisation of industrial management and some organs of state administration, on the formation of new state administration bodies, and on pensions and allowances to collective farmers, which were submitted by the Central Committee of the Party jointly with the Council of Ministers of the U.S.S.R. for consideration to the Supreme Soviet of the U.S.S.R.

The Communist Party and its Central Committee exercise its guidance of the Supreme Soviet of the U.S.S.R., as of the entire system of Soviets in the country, strictly within the framework of the Soviet Constitution. The Party and its Central Committee direct the activity of the Supreme Soviet of the U.S.S.R. through the bodies of the Supreme Soviet itself, through Communists, primarily members of the Party's Central Committee and also the Party Group in the highest legislative organ of the country. By way of illustration, the First Session of the Sixth Supreme Soviet of the U.S.S.R. elected the Presidium of the Soviet Parliament according to a motion moved by the Party Group of the Supreme Soviet and the Councils of Elders of both its chambers.

The present Party Programme and the decisions taken by the 23rd C.P.S.U. Congress call for a further development of the socialist state and of Soviet democracy. As the Party Programme indicates, the main direction in which socialist statehood develops in the period of the building of communism is all-round extension and improvement of socialist democracy, active participation of all citizens in the administration of the state and in the management of economic and cultural affairs, improvement of the government apparatus, and increased people's control over its activity.

The 23rd Party Congress outlined the ways and means of improving the work of the Supreme Soviet in discharging its broad functions as prescribed by the Soviet Constitution.

The Soviet Parliament performs its duties solely for the benefit of the working people of the country.

ELECTIONS TO THE SUPREME SOVIET OF THE U.S.S.R.

The extent to which any representative organ may be called democratic largely depends on the manner it is elected, i.e., on the extent to which the masses participate in the elections, on the opportunities they have to nominate candidates, on how far they can express their free will in the elections and on how this is reflected in the electoral returns. The Soviet Union, where the political and economic power is vested in the working people, where there are no exploiting classes, all the necessary conditions obtain for truly free elections of organs of power.

The present system of forming the higher and local organs of state power ensures the broadest and fullest representation of all strata of the population.

The Soviet electoral system is democratic in character. The Constitution of the U.S.S.R. establishes that elections to all Soviets (the Supreme Soviet of the U.S.S.R., the Supreme Soviets of the Union and Autonomous Republics, the Soviets of the Territories, Regions and Autonomous Regions, the Soviets of the National Areas and districts, cities, townships and villages) are held on the basis of universal, equal and direct suffrage by secret ballot.

All citizens who have reached the age of 18 on the day of the elections have the right to elect with the exception of those who have been declared of unsound mind. Soviet law does not impose any restrictions on the electoral rights of the citizens due to social origin or property status, past activities or religion. Soviet citizens of all nationalities, men and women alike, enjoy equal electoral rights. There are no restrictions whatsoever on the franchise of servicemen. Soviet electoral laws do not restrict the franchise by the imposition of any qualifications, which are widely applied in the bourgeois states, such as residential, educational, property and other qualifications. In 1958, the Supreme Soviet of the U.S.S.R. abolished the partial disfranchisement applied as an additional penalty to people who had committed grave crimes.

Soviet electoral law imposes no restrictions, save the age restriction, on citizens' right to be elected to a Soviet. All citizens who have reached the age of 23 on election day are eligible for election to the Supreme Soviet of the U.S.S.R. Those who have reached the age of 21 can be elected to the Supreme Soviet of a Union or Autonomous Republic, while citizens who have reached the age of 18 can be elected to local Soviets.

Both chambers of the Supreme Soviet of the U.S.S.R.—the Soviet of the Union and the Soviet of Nationalities—are elected by the population directly. The difference in the methods of their election stem from the tasks which the two chambers perform. The Soviet of the Union is elected by citizens voting by constituencies on the basis of one deputy per 300,000 of population, while the Soviet of Nationalities is elected by the citizens voting by Union Republics, Autonomous Republics, Autonomous Regions and National Areas on the representation basis of 32 deputies from each Union Republic, 11 deputies from each Autonomous Republic, five deputies from each Autonomous Region, and one deputy from each National Area.

The procedure for the elections to the Supreme Soviet is established by the *Regulations for Election to the Supreme Soviet of the U.S.S.R.* These Regulations were approved by a Decree of the Presidium of the Supreme Soviet of the U.S.S.R. on January 9, 1950, and were amended in December 1961.

The present procedure of elections to the Supreme Soviet of the U.S.S.R. guarantees the constitutional democratic principles of the Soviet electoral system and the undeviating observance of citizens' rights during the preparations for and holding of the elections.

In 1961, some changes were introduced into the Regulations for Election to the Supreme Soviet of the U.S.S.R. In particular, the rate of forming polling stations in the country underwent a change. According to the amended Regulations, polling stations are set up at large railway stations and airports; for the period of the election campaign the chairman or secretary of the primary election commission is relieved of his official duties at his or her place of regular

Meeting of the Central Election Commission for the election to the Supreme Soviet of the U.S.S.R., May 1966

ELECTIONS TO THE SUPREME SOVIET OF THE U.S.S.R.

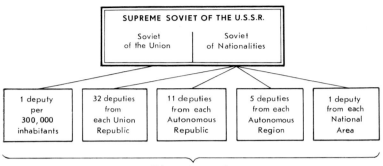

SUPREME SOVIET OF THE U.S.S.R.

Soviet of the Union | Soviet of Nationalities

| 1 deputy per 300,000 inhabitants | 32 deputies from each Union Republic | 11 deputies from each Autonomous Republic | 5 deputies from each Autonomous Region | 1 deputy from each National Area |

Electorate

employment. Moreover, the legal norms determining penalties for crimes involving the violation of citizens' electoral rights were removed from the Regulations because this question had been settled by the criminal codes adopted by the Union Republics. In March 1966, the Supreme Soviet of the U.S.S.R. increased the representation quota of the Union Republics in the Soviet of Nationalities from 25 to 32 deputies. In response to the wishes expressed by the working people and their organisations, the Presidium of the Supreme Soviet of the U.S.S.R. decreed that polling shall take place on election day from 6 a.m. to 10 p.m. local time and not to 12 p.m., as had been the case in the past.

According to the Constitution of the U.S.S.R., elections to the Supreme Soviet (both the Soviet of the Union and the Soviet of Nationalities) are conducted by constituencies. Each constituency elects only one deputy. Constituencies for elections to the Soviet of the Union and the Soviet of Nationalities are formed by the Presidium of the Supreme Soviet of the U.S.S.R. strictly in keeping with the constitutional representation quotas.

Constituencies for elections to the Soviet of the Union are formed throughout the territory of the U.S.S.R., each constituency having an equal number of inhabitants—300,000. The number of constituencies for elections to the Soviet of the Union is on the increase, due to the growth of the country's population: between 1950 and 1966 the number of Soviet of the Union constituencies rose by 99 and now totals 767. There has been a particular marked increase in the number of these constituencies in areas where giant projects are located and virgin land is developed. For instance, in Kazakhstan the number of Soviet of the Union constituencies rose from 28 to 39.

As regards constituencies in the elections to the Soviet of Nationalities, they are formed on the territorial principle of the representation of the Union and Autonomous Republics and Autonomous Regions. The territory of these republics and regions is divided into constituencies according to the constitutional representation quota. Within a Union or Autonomous Republic and an Autonomous Region these constituencies are equal in size of the population in them. The territory of a National Area comprises a constituency for elections to the Soviet of Nationalities. Since Soviet of Nationalities constituencies are formed on the basis of the representation of the Union and Autonomous Republics, Autonomous Regions and National Areas, their number in the past changed in connection with the increase of the number of the national state formations or with the change in the status of some of them (for instance, when an Autonomous Region was reorganised into an Autonomous Republic). This explains the relative stability of the number of the constituencies for elections to the Soviet of Nationalities: in 1950, 638 constituencies were formed; in 1954—639; in 1958—640; and in 1962—652.

Inasmuch as in the Soviet of Nationalities the representation quota of the Union Republics increased in 1966, the number of Soviet of Nationalities constituencies rose substantially to the present figure of 750.

Constituencies are formed by the Presidium of the Supreme Soviet of the U.S.S.R. at each election. This enables state agencies to take timely account of the changes in the numerical strength of the population in constituencies and to prevent the long existence of constituencies with an unequal number of inhabitants.

When setting up constituencies for elections both to the Soviet of the Union and the Soviet of Nationalities, the Presidium of the Supreme Soviet takes into account the country's existing administrative and territorial division and also the possibilities for organising electoral canvassing, and for assisting deputies in their day-to-day work.

The lists of constituencies with reference material on their boundaries, and so forth, are published in the press not later than two months before polling day.

For the purpose of securing the participation of all citizens in the elections to the Supreme Soviet of the U.S.S.R., the territory of constituencies is divided into polling stations.

Polling stations are common both for the election to the Soviet of the Union and to the Soviet of Nationalities. Under the Regulations for Election to the Supreme Soviet of the U.S.S.R. polling stations are set up on the basis of one per 500 to 3,000 inhabitants. Separate polling stations may be set up for a village with a population of over 100 inhabitants. In remote Northern or Eastern regions and mountainous regions, polling stations may be formed for a population of less than 100, but not under 50 inhabitants. On the islands of the Far North or at polar stations, polling stations may be set up for a population of less than 50 but not under 25. Polling stations are formed to cover the entire population of a constituency. The constituency boundaries are made known to the public through the press. Polling stations are also set up in military units or military formations with not less than 50 and not more than 3,000 electors. In addition, such stations are formed at hospitals, maternity homes, sanatoria and homes for invalids with not less than 50 electors. Stations for the receipt of ballot papers are also set up on vessels at sea on election day, on long-distance passenger trains, at large railway junctions, sea ports and airports.

In 1966, a total of over 160,000 polling stations was set up for the elections to the Supreme Soviet of the U.S.S.R. The present procedure of forming polling stations ensures the implementation of universal suffrage, enabling each elector to vote to the Supreme Soviet of the U.S.S.R.

Electoral registers. The constitutional principles of the Soviet electoral system find their reflection in the procedure of compiling electoral registers as well. Under the Regulations for Election to the Supreme Soviet of the U.S.S.R. these registers are drawn up in towns by the Executive Committees of Soviets of Working People's Deputies; in cities divided into wards, by the Executive Committees of the Ward Soviets, in townships, by the Executive Committees of

Leonid Brezhnev meeting his electors in the Kremlin Palace of Congresses on June 10, 1966

Township Soviets; and in villages, by the Executive Committees of the Village Soviets. Electoral registers are drawn up in the form approved by the Presidium of the Supreme Soviet of the U.S.S.R. and include all voters who are resident permanently or temporarily on the territory of the relevant Soviet. An elector may be listed only in one register. This serves to ensure the complete equality of the electors during elections.

Electors are entered on registers without any applications on their part. All that is required of them is that they actually reside on the territory of a Soviet.

An important guarantee of the proper compilation of the electoral registers is the duty of the Executive Committees of Soviets, which draw up these registers to exhibit them for public inspection thirty days prior to the election. Under the afore-mentioned Regulations, every elector has every possibility of checking up whether the registers had been correctly drawn up or of ascertaining data regarding himself or any other voter. An elector who finds any irregularity on a register (incorrect inclusion or exclusion, distortion of name, wrong registration, and so on) is entitled to submit an application to the Executive Committee of a Soviet which drew up the register. Should he disagree with the decision of the Executive Committee, he may file a complaint with the district (or town) people's court. The preliminary posting of electoral registers for public inspection is an effective form of people's control over the proper compilation of registers.

The simultaneous exhibition of registers for public inspection throughout the U.S.S.R. is also of great importance. Electors who for various reasons change their place of residence receive a Voting Right Certificate. The form of this document is prescribed by the Presidium of the Supreme Soviet of the U.S.S.R. When an elector is issued this certificate, a note that he has departed is made against his name on the register. Upon the presentation of the Voting Right Certificate and his identity card the elector is entered on the register at his new place of residence, or the place where he is staying on election day.

The present procedure of forming constituencies and polling stations and of compiling electoral registers enables every elector to take part in the elections to the Supreme Soviet of the U.S.S.R. This is seen from the solid participation of the electorate in the elections to the Soviet Parliament. (See table on p. 27.)

Election commissions play a big role in preparing and holding elections. They register candidates and organise voting. They are truly mass organs of the working people and consist of representatives of mass organisations, associations and societies. This can be seen, for instance, from the number of members elected to the election commissions set up for the last elections to the Supreme Soviet of the U.S.S.R. In 1966 these commissions had a total of 1,305,000 members.

Date of election	Total number of electors	Total who voted	Per cent
December 12, 1937	94,138,159	91,113,153	96.79
February 10, 1946	101,717,686	101,450,936	99.74
March 12, 1950	111,116,373	111,090,010	99.98
March 14, 1954	120,750,816	120,727,826	99.98
March 16, 1958	133,836,325	133,796,091	99.97
March 18, 1962	140,022,359	139,957,809	99.95
June 12, 1966	144,000,973	143,917,031	99.94

The elections to the Supreme Soviet of the U.S.S.R. are conducted by the following election commissions: the Central Election Commission, the Election Commissions for elections to the Soviet of Nationalities set up in the Union and Autonomous Republics, Autonomous Regions and National Areas, the District Election Commissions for elections to the Soviet of Nationalities, and also primary election commissions.

The Central Election Commission is composed of 27 representatives of mass organisations and societies (a chairman, vice-chairman, secretary and 24 members). Its membership is approved by the Presidium of the Supreme Soviet of the U.S.S.R. not later than 50 days prior to the date fixed for the elections.

The Central Election Commission is common to the elections to the Soviet of the Union and the Soviet of Nationalities. It sees to it that the Regulations for Election to the Supreme Soviet of the U.S.S.R. are strictly observed throughout the country, examines complaints concerning irregularities on the part of election commissions and takes final decisions on complaints. It approves the form and colour of ballot-papers, the form of the official records of the District and primary election commissions, and the form of election certificates, establishes standard ballot-boxes and the designs of seals for the election commissions. It is charged with the registration of the deputies elected to the Supreme Soviet of the U.S.S.R. and turns over the election files and records to the Credentials Committees of the two chambers of the Supreme Soviet of the U.S.S.R. In line with these duties, the Central Election Commission instructs other election commissions on the organisational aspects of the preparations for and the conduct of elections and interprets, when necessary, the procedures provided for by the Electoral Regulations. Regarding matters requiring a legislative solution the Central Election Commission submits its proposals to the Presidium of the Supreme Soviet of the U.S.S.R. For instance, in 1966 this Commission urged the Presidium of the Supreme Soviet to adopt a decision governing the voting procedure for the electors who, on election day, are in remote regions or regions difficult of access, or belong to scientific expeditions or geological survey parties or any other body, and who by virtue of poor means of communication are unable to go to a polling station. Accordingly, primary election commissions were authorised to organise on-the-spot voting for the afore-mentioned groups of electors, provided their group consists of not less than three electors.

Each Union or Autonomous Republic, Autonomous Region and National Area set up commissions for the election of the Soviet of Nationalities not later than 50 days before polling day. These commissions are composed of a chairman, vice-chairman, secretary and from 10 to 16 members. Their composition is approved by the Presidiums of the Supreme Soviets of the Union or Autonomous Republics or the Executive Committees of the Soviets of the Autonomous Regions, or National Areas. Their duty is to secure the proper representation of the respective national state formations in the Soviet of Nationalities. They make sure that the Electoral Regulations are strictly observed during the election of deputies to the Soviet of Nationalities from the Union or Autonomous Republics, Autonomous Regions and National Areas. They also deal with complaints of irregularities on the part of other commissions for elections to the Soviet of Nationalities.

District Election Commissions are set up in each Soviet of the Union constituency not later than 50 days before polling day. They are composed of 11 members. In Republics divided into territories and regions the District Election Commissions for elections to the Soviet of the Union are approved by the respective Executive Committees of Territory and Regional Soviets, and in Republics not divided into territories and regions—by the Presidiums of the Supreme Soviets of these Republics. The District Election Commissions for elections to the Soviet of Nationalities are approved by the Presidiums of the Supreme Soviets of the respective Union and Autonomous Republics, or by the Executive Committees of the Soviets of the Autonomous Regions and National Areas.

The electors of a constituency secure the proper election of their representative to the Supreme Soviet of the U.S.S.R. through the District Election Commission. The latter registers candidates nominated in the constituency, counts the votes cast and establishes the returns and issues a certificate of election to the elected deputy. The District Election Commissions see to it that the Electoral Regulations are strictly adhered to during elections, deal with complaints or irregularities on the part of primary election commissions and take appropriate decisions, supervise the timely formation of polling stations and the compilation of electoral registers, and supply the primary election commissions with ballot-papers. The District Election Commissions for elections to the Soviet of Nationalities turn over the election files and records to the Election Commission of the Union or Autonomous Republic, Autonomous Region or National Area, set up for elections to the Soviet of Nationalities, whereas the District Election Commissions for elections to the Soviet of the Union turn these documents over to the Central Election Commission.

A primary election commission is common for the elections to the Soviet of the Union and the Soviet of Nationalities and is formed at each polling station not later than 40 days before polling day. It consists of from three to 11 members. Primary election commissions set up at polling stations on board vessels at sea, at railway junctions or in river and sea ports may have a larger membership. The primary election commission is approved by the Executive Committee of the respective District, Town or Ward Soviet.

These commissions deal with claims concerning errors in the electoral registers and submit them for consideration to the Executive Committee of the Soviet that published the register. The chief duty of the primary commissions is to organise voting on polling day. The Electoral Regulations entrust these commissions with receiving ballot-papers and counting the votes cast at each polling station. These commissions turn over their election files and records to the respective commissions for elections to the Soviet of the Union or to the Soviet of Nationalities.

Y. Linnik, a veteran worker of the Arsenal Plant, now a pensioner, with his family at a polling station in Kiev

The present system of commissions charged with the preparation and conduct of elections covers organs composed of the representatives from mass organisations, societies, and working people's collectives, in other words, from the entire electorate. This testifies to the fact that elections to the Supreme Soviet of the U.S.S.R. are organised, conducted and controlled by the people. It is noteworthy that there has never been a case of invalidating elections on account of violations of the Electoral Regulations.

The election commissions settle their most important questions at their sittings. Experience shows that the Central Election Commission holds seven or eight sittings during its term of office and manages to consider all the crucial issues of the electoral campaign, the voting of electors and the counting of the votes.

The Electoral Regulations stipulate that all questions in the Election Commissions are decided by a simple majority vote. In the event of an equal division among its members, the chairman has the casting vote. Meetings of a commission are deemed valid provided more than one-half of its total membership is in attendance.

Nomination of candidates. Under the Constitution of the U.S.S.R., every citizen who has reached the age of 23 is eligible for election to the Supreme Soviet of the U.S.S.R. Pursuant to the Electoral Regulations, the right to nominate candidates is vested in a large number of mass organisations and societies of working people, as represented by their central, republican, territory, regional and district organs. This right is also enjoyed by general meetings of workers in enterprises and institutions, servicemen in army and naval units, peasants on collective farms, and of farm workers on state farms. In actual practice candidates are nominated exclusively by general meetings.

Candidates may be named at such meetings by local bodies of mass organisations or by individual electors. Thereupon each candidate is discussed by those present at the meeting. If a proposed candidate is not generally approved, other candidates may be nominated.

Candidates are discussed by the electors of the constituency in which they stand. Comprehensive discussion and selection of the best candidates are the main principles of the nomination of candidates for all the representative bodies of the Soviet state, thus enabling the people to send to the Soviets their finest representatives who can implement their will.

Of great importance for the selection of a candidate is the constituency pre-election meeting. It is here that representatives from mass organisations and working people's collectives of the constituency in question come to agreement following the discussion of all the nominated candidates and decide on which of these candidates to support. Candidates who did not receive support at a constituency pre-election meeting withdraw by themselves, or they are withdrawn by the organisations who nominated them.

The Soviet electoral legislation does not preclude the possibility of the nomination and balloting of several candidates in one constituency. In practice, however, one candidate stands in each constituency. The Communist Party of the Soviet Union, which expresses the interests of the entire Soviet people, nominates candidates jointly with non-Party people. This bloc of Communists and non-Party people enjoys the unanimous support of the entire population.

Organisations nominating a candidate must register him with the respective District Election Commission not later than 30 days prior to the date of the election. He is registered on the basis of the minutes of the meeting at which he was nominated either by a local mass organisation or by the staff of an enterprise or establishment. He may be registered with the election commission only on the proviso that he has given his consent in writing to stand for election in the constituency in question on behalf of the organisations nominating him. In the relevant constituency the registered candidate is entered on the ballot-papers, which also bear the name of the organisation nominating him.

A person may be registered as a candidate for election to either chamber of the Supreme Soviet of the U.S.S.R., but in one constituency only.

The Electoral Regulations provide that candidates for the Supreme Soviet of the U.S.S.R. may not be members of the district or primary election commissions in the constituency in which they were nominated. If a candidate turns out to be on the afore-mentioned commission, he must be forthwith released from his duties as a member of the commission.

The success of every electoral campaign depends largely on the organisation of canvassing. According to the Electoral Regulations, the District Election Commission publishes the relevant data (the full name, age, occupation, Party affiliation, and so on) concerning the registered candidate not later than 25 days prior to the date of the election. Every organisation which has nominated a candidate and likewise every citizen of the U.S.S.R. is ensured with the right of freely canvassing in favour of that candidate. The Government places all mass media at the disposal of the working people, including the press, radio and television. The electors are ensured with broad possibilities for acquainting themselves with their candidates at special meetings with the latter, through election posters, the bio graphies of candidates posted in the streets and the appeals by district pre-election meetings of the authorised representatives of mass organisations.

Voting procedure. Nearly all Soviet electors vote for candidates of the people's bloc of Communists and non-Party people. This is

Date of election to the Supreme Soviet	Votes cast for deputies to the Soviet of the Union	Per cent of the total electorate	Votes cast for deputies to the Soviet of Nationalities	Per cent of the total electorate
December 12, 1937	89,844,271	98.61	89,063,169	97.75
February 10, 1946	100,621,225	99.18	100,603,567	99.16
March 12, 1950	110,788,377	99.73	110,782,009	99.72
March 14, 1954	120,479,249	99.79	120,539,860	99.84
March 16, 1958	133,214,652	99.57	133,431,524	99.73
March 18, 1962	139,210,431	99.47	139,391,455	99.60
June 12, 1966	143,570,976	99.76	143,595,678	99.80

shown by the returns of the elections to the Supreme Soviet of the U.S.S.R. over the last 20 years. (See table above.)

Soviet electoral legislation provides all the necessary conditions for the participation of every elector in the elections to the Supreme Soviet of the U.S.S.R. Elections are held on off-days. The Presidium of the Supreme Soviet of the U.S.S.R. issues its Decree on the date of the polling day at least 60 days in advance. Over a period of 20 days preceding the election day, the primary election commissions are obliged to make the date and place of polling known to the electors.

Polling takes place on election day from 6 a.m. to 10 p.m. local time. It cannot be terminated before 10 p.m., even if all the electors entered on the registers have cast their vote. This is due to the fact that a polling station may be used by electors possessing a Voting Right Certificate. Every elector votes personally, going to the polling station for this purpose. Voters unable to come to the polling station because of illness or for any other good reason may cast their votes by dropping their ballot-papers in the ballot-boxes brought to their home.

The present voting procedure provides every elector with the real possibility of freely expressing his own will in the elections. Voters cast their votes by depositing their ballot-papers in the ballot-box. If the elector votes for a candidate, he leaves the name of the candidate on the ballot-paper; if he votes against him, he crosses his name out. Every voter is ensured with secrecy of voting. Private booths or special rooms are set aside on the premises of polling stations for the purpose of filling in ballot-papers. No person, not even members of the primary election commission, with the exception of the voter filling in his ballot-paper, may be present in these booths or rooms at polling time. Any violation of the secrecy of voting is a crime under Soviet law.

To ensure full freedom of voting, the Electoral Regulations do not permit electioneering at the polling station on election day.

The present voting procedure is so organised as to disperse the slightest doubt regarding the proper results of the elections. Before polling, the chairman of a primary election commission, in the presence of the members of the commission, closes the ballot-boxes and seals them with the commission seal. Prior to the termination of polling the ballot-boxes may not be opened and the votes cast may not be counted.

To preclude any possibility of an elector voting more than once, special entries are made on the electoral register against the name of the voter who received his ballot-paper. The voters who appear on the election premises with an Election Right Certificate are entered on an additional roll.

Upon the termination of polling at 10 p.m., the primary election commission proceeds to count the votes cast. Before opening the ballot-boxes, the commission seals all the unused ballot-papers with its seal. The members of the election commission apart, representatives of mass organisations and societies of working people, specially authorised for the purpose, and also representatives of the press have the right to attend the counting of the votes cast. The results of the vote are duly entered into the official record. The primary election commission dispatches by messenger one copy of the official record to the respective District Commission which on the basis of these records makes a count of the votes for the constituency. The can-

Baku electors make merry on polling day

didate who receives more than one-half the total number of valid votes cast in the constituency is deemed elected. Elections are deemed valid if more than half the total electorate resident in the given constituency have taken part in the election. The returns for the election in a constituency are entered by the election commission into an official voting record. Representatives of mass organisations and societies of working people and of the press have also the right to be present on the premises where the votes cast are being counted by a District Election Commission.

On the basis of the official voting records submitted by the District Election Commissions, the Central Election Commission counts the votes cast and announces the returns for the whole country, and also compiles a list of the deputies elected to the Supreme Soviet of the U.S.S.R. The returns and the list of the newly-elected deputies are published by the Central Election Commission in the press.

All the materials received from the District Election Commissions the Central Election Commission turns over to the Credentials Committees of the Soviet of the Union and the Soviet of Nationalities, which are elected at the first session of the Supreme Soviet of the U.S.S.R. These Committees report on the results of the verification of the credentials of the newly-elected deputies to the respective chambers, which approve or disapprove the credentials, as the case may be.

DEPUTIES ARE REPRESENTATIVES OF THE PEOPLE

The Soviet deputy is a true representative of the working people in the Soviets. The deputies elected to both chambers of the Supreme Soviet of the U.S.S.R. are distributed in the following way:

Convocation	Soviet of the Union	Soviet of Nationalities	Total
January 1937	569	574	1,143
February 1946	682	657	1,339
March 1950	678	638	1,316
April 1954	708	639	1,347
May 1958	738	640	1,378
June 1962	791	652	1,443
July 1966	767	750	1,517

The diagram below shows the representation quota of the Union and Autonomous Republics, Autonomous Regions and National Areas in the Soviet of Nationalities.

Convocation	Deputies from Union Republics	Deputies from Autonomous Republics	Deputies from Autonomous Regions	Deputies from National Areas
January 1937	275	242	45	12
February 1946	400	176	45	10
March 1950	400	176	45	10
April 1954	400	176	45	10
May 1958	375	198	50	10
June 1962	375	220	40	10
July 1966	480	220	40	10

The deputies of the Supreme Soviet of the U.S.S.R. represent all sections of the people. The Seventh Supreme Soviet members include 404 factory workers, or 26.6 per cent of the total deputy body, and 294 collective farmers, or 19.4 per cent. Three hundred and fifty-eight members of the Soviet of the Union, or 46.7 per cent, and 340 members of the Soviet of Nationalities, or 45.3 per cent, are directly employed in production.

Members of the Seventh Supreme Soviet of the U.S.S.R. According to Occupation and Branch of Industry:

	Soviet of the Union	Per cent	Soviet of Nationalities	Per cent	Both Chambers	Per cent
1. Factory, building, transport and communications workers	228	29.7	151	20.1	379	25.0
of whom:						
workers (foremen and team leaders)	185	24.1	124	16.5	309	20.4
including						
machine-builders	51	6.7	36	4.8	87	5.7
miners, oil-men, metal-workers and chemists	63	8.2	35	4.7	98	6.5
builders	20	2.6	16	2.1	36	2.4
railway workers	13	1.7	7	0.9	20	1.3
textile workers, workers of the sewing industry, shoemakers	31	4.0	20	2.7	51	3.4
workers from other industries	7	0.9	10	1.3	17	1.1
industrial executives and specialists	43	5.6	27	3.6	70	4.6
2. Agriculturists,	181	23.6	229	30.5	410	27.0
including						
state-farm workers	35	4.6	60	8.0	95	6.3
managers of state farms, pedigree stud farms and specialists	8	1.0	13	1.7	21	1.4
collective farmers,	138	18.0	156	20.8	294	19.4
including						
collective-farm chairmen	53	6.9	46	6.1	99	6.5
3. Scientists, workers engaged in culture, literature or the arts	70	9.1	84	11.2	154	10.2
of whom:						
workers of the U.S.S.R. Academy of Sciences, Academies of the Union Republics and other academies	19	2.5	13	1.7	32	2.1
rectors, heads of chairs and teachers of institutes	13	1.7	6	0.8	19	1.2
headmasters and school-teachers	9	1.2	13	1.7	22	1.5

	Soviet of the Union	Per cent	Soviet of Nationalities	Per cent	Both Chambers	Per cen
doctors	9	1.2	12	1.6	21	1.4
writers	12	1.6	14	1.9	26	1.7
actors	4	0.5	8	1.0	12	0.8
composers	1	0.1	5	0.7	6	0.4
artists	1	0.1	3	0.4	4	0.3
journalists, publishers, etc.	2	0.3	4	0.5	6	0.4
workers from other organisations	—	—	6	0.8	6	0.4
4. Workers of Party, trade union and Y.C.L. bodies	160	20.9	129	17.2	289	19.1
5. Workers of Soviets	98	12.8	131	17.5	229	15.1
of whom:						
President and Secretary of the Presidium of the Supreme Soviet of the U.S.S.R., Chairman and Vice-Chairmen of the Council of Ministers of the U.S.S.R., Ministers of the U.S.S.R. and Chairmen of State Committees	43	5.6	47	6.3	90	5.9
Presidents of the Presidiums of the Supreme Soviets of the Union Republics	1	0.1	14	1.8	15	1.0
Chairmen, Vice-Chairmen of the Councils of Ministers of the Union Republics	26	3.4	41	5.5	67	4.4
Chairmen of the Councils of Ministers of the Autonomous Republics	5	0.7	13	1.7	18	1.2
Chairmen of the Executive Committees of local Soviets	23	3.0	16	2.1	39	2.6
6. Servicemen	30	3.9	26	3.5	56	3.7

There are 425 women (28 per cent of the total) in the Seventh Supreme Soviet of the U.S.S.R. This figure exceeds the total number of women elected to the parliaments in all the capitalist countries put together.

Of the 222 women elected to the Soviet of the Union, 112 are workers, engineers or technicians employed in various branches of

Soviet Premier Alexei Kosygin makes a government policy statement to the Seventh Supreme Soviet of the U.S.S.R. on August 3, 1966

industry and agriculture, 25 are scientists or cultural workers or leading functionaries in the Soviets. They include prominent workers engaged in industry and agriculture: Heroes of Socialist Labour T. Akhunova, G. A. Borzova, M. A. Bryntseva, S. D. Vishtak, S. M. Gasanova, M. Zhanybayeva, S. T. Palvinskaya, K. K. Petukhova, Z. P. Pukhova, E. B. Solomoniya; G. M. Gasparyan, People's Artist of the U.S.S.R.; A. I. Kasatkina, member of the Presidium of the Supreme Soviet of the U.S.S.R.; D. P. Komarova, Chairman of the Executive Committee of the Bryansk Regional Soviet; V. V. Nikolayeva-Tereshkova, cosmonaut; Y. A. Furtseva, Minister of Culture of the U.S.S.R.; Prof. T. V. Shlopak, and others.

Of the 203 women elected to the Soviet of Nationalities 48 are industrial workers, 34 are agriculturists, 30 are educationalists or public health workers, five are chairmen of the Executive Committees of local Soviets, two are Secretaries of the Y.C.L. of the Union Republics, 13 are teachers, 11 are doctors, and four are actors. The members of the Soviet of Nationalities include Y. S. Nasriddinova, President of the Presidium of the Supreme Soviet of the Uzbek Republic; T. N. Nikolayeva, Secretary of the All-Union Central Council of Trade Unions; B. Bultrikova, Vice-Chairman of the Council of Ministers of the Kazakh Republic; Z. I. Guseinova, Minister of

Higher and Secondary Specialised Education of the Azerbaijan Republic; T. V. Lashkarashvili, Minister of Education of the Georgian Republic; A. D. Nutetegryneh, Member of the Presidium of the Supreme Soviet of the U.S.S.R. There are many production innovators among the deputies, including Heroes of Socialist Labour T. R. Aliyeva, L. E. Barakhoeva, N. I. Vorobyova, M. N. Kapusta, G. A. Kizelene, L. Lee, U. Milikulova, P. S. Muntyan, L. I. Osiyuk, B. M. Talybova, A. M. Formanyuk, and A. A. Shulimova.

Members of the Seventh Supreme Soviet of the U.S.S.R. According to Party Affiliation:

	Soviet of the Union	Per cent	Soviet of Nationalities	Per cent	Both Chambers	Per cent
Members and candidate members of the C.P.S.U.	573	74.7	568	75.7	1,141	75.2
Non-Party people	194	25.3	182	24.3	376	24.8

The multinational composition of the Supreme Soviet of the U.S.S.R. reflects the unbreakable friendship among the Soviet peoples and is conclusive proof that all nations and nationalities inhabiting the country enjoy genuine equality. Fifty-eight nationalities are represented in the Supreme Soviet of U.S.S.R.

All these nationalities are represented in the Soviet Parliament as follows:

Nationality	Soviet of the Union	Soviet of Nationalities	Both Chambers
Russians	454	191	645
Ukrainians	141	59	200
Byelorussians	24	32	56
Uzbeks	27	25	52
Kazakhs	17	19	36
Georgians	11	39	50
Azerbaijanians	11	36	47
Lithuanians	9	23	32
Moldavians	2	20	22
Letts	4	24	28
Kirghizes	3	20	23
Tajiks	6	29	35
Armenians	9	39	48
Turkmen	5	22	27
Estonians	3	26	29
Abkhazians	1	6	7

Nationality	Soviet of the Union	Soviet of Nationalities	Both Chambers
Bashkirs	4	5	9
Buryats	2	7	9
Avars	2	2	4
Darghins	—	3	3
Kumyks	—	2	2
Laks	—	1	1
Lezghins	1	2	3
Kabardinians	1	5	6
Balkars	1	2	3
Kalmyks	—	6	6
Kara-Kalpaks	—	5	5
Karelians	1	5	6
Komi	2	7	9
Mari	1	4	5
Mordvinians	2	5	7
Ossets	3	11	14
Tatars	7	11	18
Tuvinians	1	7	8
Udmurts	3	3	6
Chechen	1	5	6
Ingushes	1	1	2
Chuvashes	2	6	8
Yakuts	1	4	5
Adigheis	—	3	3
Altaians	—	3	3
Jews	2	3	5
Karachais	—	1	1
Circassians	—	1	1
Khakasses	—	3	3
Nentsi	—	2	2
Chukchi	—	1	1
Evenks	—	2	2
Evens	—	1	1
Abazians	—	1	1
Uighurs	—	1	1
Dolganians	—	1	1
Khanty	—	1	1
Bulgars	—	1	1
Gagauzes	1	—	1
Koreans	—	1	1
Poles	1	4	5
Finns	—	1	1

Age Composition of the Seventh Supreme Soviet of the U.S.S.R.
(at the time of election)

Age	Soviet of the Union	Per cent	Soviet of Nationalities	Per cent	Both Chambers	Per cent
Under 30	87	11.3	95	12.6	182	12.0
31 to 40	204	26.6	230	30.7	434	28.6
41 to 50	210	27.4	210	28.0	420	27.7
51 to 60	228	29.7	158	21.1	386	25.4
Over 61	38	5.0	57	7.6	95	6.3

Educational Composition of the Seventh Supreme Soviet of the U.S.S.R.

Education	Soviet of the Union	Per cent	Soviet of Nationalities	Per cent	Both Chambers	Per cent
Primary	38	5.0	52	6.9	90	5.9
Incomplete secondary	186	24.2	158	21.1	344	22.7
Secondary	141	18.4	134	17.9	275	18.1
Incomplete higher	22	2.9	25	3.3	47	3.1
Higher	380	49.5	381	50.8	761	50.2

Members of the Seventh Supreme Soviet of the U.S.S.R. with Special Qualifications:

Trade or profession	Soviet of the Union	Per cent	Soviet of Nationalities	Per cent	Both Chambers	Per cent
Total,	438	57.1	435	58.0	873	57.6
of whom:						
Engineers and technicians	182	23.7	129	17.2	311	20.5
Agronomists, zoo-technicians and other farm specialists	99	12.9	78	10.4	177	11.7
Economists	4	0.5	12	1.6	16	1.1
Doctors	19	2.5	14	1.9	33	2.2
Lawyers	4	0.5	10	1.3	14	0.9
Teachers	45	5.9	87	11.6	132	8.7
Other specialists	85	11.1	105	14.0	190	12.5

Deputies to the Seventh Supreme Soviet of the U.S.S.R. include:
Members of the Academy of Sciences of the U.S.S.R.—21
Corresponding Members of the Academy of Sciences of the
U.S.S.R. —14

Members of the Academies of Union Republics   —24
Corresponding Members of the Academies of Union Republics—8
Members and Corresponding Members of other Academies—13
    Seventy-four deputies hold the academic degree of Doctor of
Sciences, and 49 deputies—Candidate of Sciences.
    An idea of the number of distinguished men and women who have
been returned to the Seventh Supreme Soviet of the U.S.S.R. is given
in the following table:

	Soviet of the Union	Soviet of Nationalities	Both Chambers
Heroes of the Soviet Union	22	20	42
Heroes of Socialist Labour	98	91	189
Lenin and State prize winners	64	69	133

    A total of 1,163 men and women, or 76.7 per cent of the Seventh
Supreme Soviet deputies, were decorated with orders and medals.
    Of the 1,517 members of the Soviet Parliament, 992 (474 deputies
in the Soviet of the Union and 518 deputies in the Soviet of Nationalities), or 65.4 per cent, were elected to the Supreme Soviet of
the U.S.S.R. for the first time.
    Deputies take an active part in the all-round activities of the Sup-
reme Soviet: in its regular meetings, in the meetings of the chambers' standing committees, in the formation of other committees of
the Supreme Soviet, in preparations for its sessions, in the interpretation and realisation of decisions passed by the Supreme Soviet.
    Any deputy may be elected to leading bodies of the Soviet of the
Union and the Soviet of Nationalities, to the Presidium of the
Supreme Soviet of the U.S.S.R., to the standing committees of both
its chambers. Every deputy discharges his duty by taking an active
part in the deliberations of all these bodies. The First Session of the
Seventh Supreme Soviet of the U.S.S.R. appointed deputies to the
following posts or elected others to the following bodies:

	Soviet of the Union	Soviet of Nationalities	Total
Chairmen or Vice-Chairmen of the chambers	5	5	10
Members of Standing Committees of the chambers	350	350	700
Members of the Presidium of the Supreme Soviet of the U.S.S.R.	19	17	36
Members of the Soviet Government	45	41	86

ORGANISATION OF WORK IN THE SUPREME SOVIET OF THE U.S.S.R.

Sessions

Supreme Soviet sessions, the supreme assembly of representatives of the Soviet people, are one of the basic forms of activity of the Soviet Parliament. These sessions consider major problems of political, economic, social and cultural development, lay down the basic line for the home and foreign policies of the Soviet Government, debate bills and pass laws; they elect the Presidium of the Supreme Soviet, form the Government, elect the Supreme Court of the U.S.S.R., appoint the Procurator-General of the U.S.S.R., and scrutinise reports submitted by subordinate bodies.

The Sixth Supreme Soviet (at its five sessions) and the Seventh Supreme Soviet (so far at its two sessions) discussed the annual state economic development plans, the state budgets of the U.S.S.R., and the reports on the execution of the budgets. The Supreme Soviet also reviewed ways and means of improving industrial management, which is of paramount importance for the country. In the period 1962-1967, it passed the Law on Pensions and Allowances to Collective-Farm Members, the Law on the Increase of Wages to Workers Employed in Education, Health Protection, Housing and Communal Services, Trade and Public Catering and in Other Sectors of the Economy Catering for the Population.

It adopted a decision concerning the elaboration of a new Draft Constitution of the U.S.S.R. and complemented the membership of the Constitutional Commission charged by the Seventh Supreme Soviet with drafting the new Fundamental Law of the country.

Foreign policy issues occupied a place of pride in the work of the Supreme Soviet in this period. It debated the foreign policy reports submitted by the Government; deputies addressed questions to the Minister of Foreign Affairs and debated his answers. On the initiative of the two Committees for Foreign Affairs the First Session of the Seventh Supreme Soviet of the U.S.S.R. adopted a Statement on the escalation of U.S. imperialist aggression.

Pursuant to the Constitution of the U.S.S.R. the first sessions of the Sixth and Seventh Supreme Soviets elected the Presidiums of the Supreme Soviet and appointed the Soviet Government. On August 3, 1966, the First Session of the Seventh Supreme Soviet considered the Statement made by the newly-formed Government and approved the main trends of its activity in home and foreign policies.

The deputies reviewed the questions of improving the organisation of work of the Supreme Soviet. The First Session of the Seventh Supreme Soviet scrutinised the question of standing committees in the Soviet of the Union and the Soviet of Nationalities. Both chambers set up a number of new standing committees to improve the legislation process and the verification of the execution of laws, and to enhance the activity of deputies.

According to the Constitution of the U.S.S.R., the Supreme Soviet sessions are convened by the Presidium of the Supreme Soviet of the U.S.S.R. Regular sessions take place twice a year, while extraordinary sessions are convened by the Presidium either at its own discretion or on demand of one of the Union Republics.

As a rule, the Presidium of the Supreme Soviet of the U.S.S.R. publishes its decree on the convocation of a Supreme Soviet session 20-30 days before the session begins. In the interval between sessions, the Presidium of the Supreme Soviet of the U.S.S.R. concentrates all the materials to be submitted for consideration by the Supreme Soviet of the U.S.S.R. Therefore, when the Presidium sets the date of a session, it sums up the proposals at hand and selects problems to be submitted to the deputies, who decide what problems to put on the agenda.

As a rule, the chambers hold separate sittings, but in certain cases they hold joint sittings. Under the Constitution of the U.S.S.R., joint sittings of the Soviet of the Union and the Soviet of Nationalities are held to elect the Presidium of the Supreme Soviet and to form the Soviet Government—the Council of Ministers of the U.S.S.R. Joint sittings may be also convened by decision of the chambers themselves. Chiefly this is done to hear a report on the agenda to be considered and approved by both chambers. This practice is adopted when the Soviet Parliament discusses a law on the state plan for national economic development, the State Budget of the U.S.S.R., and some other matters. Though reports are heard at joint sittings, the debate on them proceeds in separate sittings of the chambers. If the deputies of both chambers deem it necessary they may decide on a joint sitting for a debate.

The sittings of each chamber are held from 10 o'clock in the morning till two o'clock in the afternoon, or from three o'clock in the afternoon till seven o'clock in the evening. This is the general rule adopted by the Seventh Supreme Soviet of the U.S.S.R. in its Standing Orders. The Orders may provide for a different time-table of sittings if the chambers decide so when they are approving their order of work.

Separate sittings of the chambers are presided over by the respective chairman, or by one of vice-chairmen on his behalf. Joint sittings of the chambers are presided over alternately by the Chairman of the Soviet of the Union and the Chairman of the Soviet of Nationalities.

Joint sitting of the two chambers of the Soviet Parliament on August 2, 1966

The deputies of both chambers elect their respective chairman and vice-chairmen at the first session of each Supreme Soviet. According to tradition, the first session of a newly-elected Supreme Soviet is inaugurated by the eldest deputy in the respective chamber. He also presides over the sitting preceding the official election of a chairman.

The agenda for each session is approved at the sittings of the respective chambers. Ordinarily, the presiding deputy announces what questions had been submitted for consideration by the Supreme Soviet at a given session. The deputies introduce their motions concerning any debated question, the order of work of the session and the inclusion of one or another question on the agenda. Thereupon the agenda is put to vote in order to elucidate the opinions of deputies.

As soon as the agenda is approved, the chambers review and decide on the appropriate sequence of points to be discussed at the session. They also decide whether to hold joint or separate sessions.

The Presidium of the Supreme Soviet and the chairmen of both chambers play a vital role in advancing motions on the order of business at a session and on the points to be included in the agenda. The motions on these questions are submitted to the Councils of Elders for their preliminary consideration.

The Councils of Elders in the chambers are a kind of conference of representatives from various groups of deputies. Their main task is to produce an agreed recommendation on the inclusion in the agenda of questions submitted for consideration at a session, on the sequence of questions to be discussed, and on the membership of the bodies which the Supreme Soviet elects.

Both chambers of the Supreme Soviet form the Councils of Elders at every new convocation. The Elders' Council of the Soviet of the Union consists of representatives from groups of deputies elected by constituencies formed on a territory of a Republic or Territory, or Region. Every group of deputies sends one representative to the Elders' Council. A group of more than 10 deputies sends two representatives, a group of more than 20 deputies sends three representatives.

The Elders' Council of the Soviet of Nationalities consists of representatives from groups of deputies, elected by every Union Republic (six representatives), by every Autonomous Republic (two representatives), and by every Autonomous Region (one representative), and also of deputies elected to the Soviet of Nationalities from the National Areas.

At present the Elders' Council of the Soviet of the Union has 157 deputies on its panel, while its counterpart in the Soviet of Nationalities has 148 deputies. The membership of both Councils reflects a cross-section of professions, including workers, collective farmers, scientists, writers, doctors, teachers, Party, government and trade union workers, and so forth. Women constitute over 20 per cent, and non-Party people about 20 per cent.

Preliminary discussions of a session's order of business in the Elders' Councils facilitate the preparation and submission of motions on these questions, with due account being taken of the opinion of a large number of deputies.

The session starts its work with the consideration of its agenda: it hears a report made by a representative of the organ which submitted the relevant question for consideration by the Supreme Soviet. The rapporteurs are approved by the chairmen of the chambers in accordance with their Standing Orders. The time allotted for a report is fixed by the chairman in consultation with rapporteurs.

The report substantiates the main points of a bill or a motion on any matter submitted for the Supreme Soviet's consideration, or brings to light the essence of the activities of a body accountable to the Supreme Soviet, as the case may be. In case there are co-rapporteurs, the chambers hear co-reports. The time for a co-report is fixed by the chairman in consultation with the co-rapporteur.

Co-reports are ordinarily presented by the chamber standing committees, which have scrutinised a bill or a motion on behalf of the chamber or the Presidium of the Supreme Soviet in the period between the sessions of the Supreme Soviet. The right to propose a co-rapporteur also belongs to a group of not less than 50 deputies.

The standing committee co-report sets forth its opinion on a question the Supreme Soviet considers and substantiates the committee motions. The preliminary scrutiny of bills and motions by the standing committees and the presentation of their opinion to the chambers in no way bind the deputies during the debate. Moreover, these procedures facilitate a thorough and comprehensive consideration of the items on the agenda and the adoption of the most reasonable decisions.

The standing committees produce recommendations to the Supreme Soviet and make co-reports on major bills and other matters. They fulfil this function when the session considers an economic development plan or a state budget. In the latter case this is specially stipulated by the 1959 Law on the Budgetary Powers of the U.S.S.R. and the Union Republics (Arts. 18 and 19).

A recommendation and a co-report of the respective standing committee are the result of collective work by a large group of deputies, and also of discussions and searches for the best solutions of specific questions. In due course the committees submit their amendments to bills, motions and remarks to the respective chamber.

Before the State Economic Development Plan and the State Budget for 1967 were approved by the Seventh Supreme Soviet of the U.S.S.R. at its Second Session in December 1966, they had been thoroughly considered by the Planning and Budgetary Committees of the two chambers and by their sectoral committees—the Committee for Industry, Transport and Communications, the Committee for Construction and the Building Materials Industry, the Committee for

Agriculture, the Committee for Public Health and Social Security, the Committee for Public Education, Science and Culture, and the Committee for Trade and Public Amenities.

The committees introduced a number of proposals to the plan and the budget. They deemed it possible to augment the plan for the production of cotton and woollen fabrics, foot-wear and other consumer goods and also proposed to increase the budgetary revenue by 120 million rubles and allocate this sum for the organisation of public services and amenities in settlements, for the supply of equipment to hospitals, schools, child welfare establishments and other social and cultural institutions and for their repairs. In addition, these committees voiced remarks and suggestions concerning the work of ministries, and planning and financial bodies.

The deputies supported the suggestions made by the standing committees concerning the plan and the budget and approved them with due account for the proposed changes. The Supreme Soviet instructed the Council of Ministers to consider the remarks and suggestions concerning ministries and departments and to take appropriate decisions on them.

One more example. Before the Fourth Session of the Sixth Supreme Soviet (July 1964) considered the bill on pensions and allowances to collective farmers, the latter had been scrutinised in advance by the Committees for Legislative Proposals, which subsequently tabled substantial amendments to it. The deputies agreed to these amendments and included them in the law.

The next stage of the Supreme Soviet deliberations is a debate. A deputy who obtains the floor to speak is given 20 minutes to express his views on a question in debate, to table motions, remarks and adduce arguments in their favour. A deputy is limited to a five minutes' statement in the chamber if he speaks for the second time.

Customarily, joint and separate sittings of both chambers are attended by over 90 per cent of all deputies. Motions are debated in a businesslike atmosphere. Reports and co-reports are discussed by deputies who represent different Republics and belong to different professions. Among them are leaders of central and local Party and government bodies, representatives of mass organisations, factory managers, industrial and agricultural experts, workers, collective farmers, teachers, doctors, scientists and workers of culture. The following examples give an idea of how debates proceed. All in all, 49 deputies took the floor in the debate on the State Economic Development Plan for 1967, the State Budget for 1967 and the report on the execution of the Budget for 1965 during the Second Session of the Seventh Supreme Soviet of the U.S.S.R. They represented all the 15 Union Republics, six Autonomous Republics, one Autonomous Region and one National Area. Among the speakers at one of the sittings of the Soviet of the Union were the Minister of Public Health of the U.S.S.R. deputy B. V. Petrovsky, the Chairman of the Council of

Ministers of the Tajik Republic deputy A. Kakharov, the First Secretary of the Volgograd Regional Party Committee deputy L. S. Kulichenko, a medical research worker from Azerbaijan and non-Party deputy Z. M. Salayeva, the captain of a Latvian fishing trawler deputy I. A. Lanki and a steelmaker from the Kuznetsk Iron and Steel Combine deputy K. F. Shabalov.

The speakers dwelt on the successes achieved, brought to light shortcomings, and criticised various departments for their omissions and mistakes in economic and cultural matters. As conscientious and prudent masters of their country, the deputies tabled interesting proposals and proved the urgency of measures aimed at strengthening Soviet economy and culture.

Deputy V. I. Prokhorov emphasised the need to improve the cost accounting principle along scientific lines and to extend its operation to every shop, sector and even every factory bench. He noted that to do this the enterprises had to give a great deal of thought to the system of intra-factory planning, operational control and the study of the most important indices of production in separate links, and the timely economic substantiation of the scale of collective and individual material incentives for the achievement of the highest results with the least expenditure.

Deputy Y. Y. Matulis highlighted the problem of training economists. He pointed to the need of synthesising the proposals advanced by Republics, ministries and departments and of tabling a proposal concerning the building of new institutes of higher learning for training economists and the equipment of laboratories with more computers.

Many of the speakers dwelt on the need to put local resources to greater use. Deputy Y. V. Ilnitsky stressed the importance of working the deposits of marble, tufa and other building materials available in the Trans-Carpathian Region. Deputy A. Klychov tabled a proposal on the greater exploitation of the oil deposits in the Turkmen Republic. Deputies M. Beisebayev, A. Kakharov and others discussed means and ways of improving the planning of capital construction.

Deputy Z. A. Fyodorova raised the question of building several schools in her constituency. She noted that schools needed more visual devices, cinema projectors, TV sets and better equipped laboratories in order to provide better instruction.

Many of the deputies criticised the work of ministries and departments. A. D. Nutetegryneh, a member of the Soviet of Nationalities, criticised the Ministry of Civil Aviation for its disregard of local airlines. This criticism impelled the Minister of Civil Aviation of the U.S.S.R. deputy Y. F. Loginov to take the floor at one of the subsequent sittings of this chamber. He reported on the measures the Ministry was planning in order to improve the local airlines.

The activity of the Supreme Soviet of the U.S.S.R. provides striking evidence that all its deputies follow deliberations with keen interest and display a businesslike approach to them. At a session held in October 1965, thirty-six members of the Sixth Supreme Soviet discussed the ways and means of improving industrial management. They tabled concrete proposals and advanced critical remarks intended for the improvement of industrial management. The deputies fully approved the proposals concerning the organisation of industrial management on a branch principle, the further improvement of planning and the strengthening of the economic incentives for industrial production.

Bearing in mind the new economic reform, they emphasised the vast importance of maintaining long-established business relations between enterprises of different industries through the newly-formed ministries, and of extending co-operation between them. They insisted that departmental barriers should not interfere with the solution of economic problems common for a region or a Republic. They made it a point that the shortcomings in the work of ministries existing before 1957 should not be repeated and that the strictly departmental approach to the problems should be uprooted.

The deputies drew the attention of the Government to the fact that the reorganisation of industrial management and the vesting of broader powers in enterprises made it imperative to improve the qualifications of factory managers and specialists and introduce a great improvement in the economic performance of enterprises, planning and economic organisations, and in the efficiency and organisation of labour in the administrative apparatus.

Proposals differ by their character and by the scale of problems raised. But, on the whole, they are the upshot of the collective experience and knowledge gained by deputies and millions of electors. This enables the deputies to work out decisions that most fully meet the needs of the people and the social progress of the country.

There is also great activity during debates. Of great importance here is the fact that upon convening a session of the supreme legislature, the Presidium of the Supreme Soviet informs the deputies in good time of the questions to be put on its agenda. Being conversant with the state of affairs in their constituencies and taking into account the opinion of electors, deputies who take the floor at sessions table concrete proposals on the business at hand and voice critical remarks on the work of central and local institutions and organisations.

The drafts of laws, decisions and other acts to be submitted for the Soviet Parliament's consideration, and also the findings of its standing committees are handed to all deputies in advance. When necessary, they are given reference materials on the questions to be debated. When they elect the Presidium of the Supreme Soviet of the U.S.S.R. or appoint the Soviet Government, they are provided with materials giving the service record of every person nominated to these bodies.

When the Supreme Soviet passes the relevant decisions it takes into consideration the proposals and remarks made by deputies at sessions. The deputies themselves decide on the order for the realisation of tabled amendments, proposals and remarks. In particular, they may instruct a specially formed committee to prepare motions on concrete amendments to a bill or any other legislative act.

Decisions are passed after the debate is terminated and the concluding speech by a rapporteur is made. Bills are voted on by chambers separately, in conformity with the Constitution of the U.S.S.R.

The first session of the Supreme Soviet of every new convocation has certain specific features which stem from the range of questions included in its agenda and to be settled in order to ensure the normal functioning of the legislature.

As we have said, the first session elects the chairmen and vice-chairmen of the chambers, and also their Credentials Committees, and hears the reports submitted by these committees on the results of the elections to the Supreme Soviet and on the verification of the credentials of the elected deputies. It also forms other standing committees. This, however, does not preclude the possibility of taking a decision to change the membership of a committee or to form a new standing committee.

The long-established procedure of nominating and discussing candidates to the posts of chairmen and vice-chairmen of the chambers, and the chairmen and members of the standing committees makes it possible to take into account all the proposals and wishes of deputies. For instance, at the First Session of the Seventh Supreme Soviet of the U.S.S.R. the relevant candidatures were proposed to the chambers by their Councils of Elders. As for the proposals concerning the membership of the standing committees and candidates for the posts of the chairmen and vice-chairmen of the two chambers, they were tabled by groups of deputies. Thus, in the Soviet of the Union the proposal on the formation and the membership of the Budgetary Committee was tabled on behalf of a group of deputies from the Ukrainian, Kazakh and Latvian Republics, and in the Soviet of Nationalities a similar proposal came from a group of the deputies from the Russian Federation and the Azerbaijan and Armenian Republics.

According to the Constitution of the U.S.S.R., the first session of the Supreme Soviet of every convocation elects, at a joint sitting of the two chambers, the Presidium of the Supreme Soviet and appoints the Council of Ministers of the U.S.S.R.

When the legislature forms its organs, elects the Presidium of the Supreme Soviet and appoints the Council of Ministers, every deputy may voice his own considerations regarding the candidates, and challenge them or nominate other candidates. The voting procedure is established by the deputies themselves. Voting may take place for each candidate separately or for the membership of an elected organ as a whole, or in any other way, as the deputies may deem it necessary.

The Supreme Soviet sittings are public, being attended by representatives from enterprises, offices and mass organisations. All official communications and other information concerning the Supreme Soviet's sittings are published in the press during its session. The official reports and speeches by deputies and also the decisions of the Supreme Soviet are likewise published in the newspapers. As soon as a session is terminated, a verbatim report of its materials is issued in the languages of all the Union Republics.

Auxiliary Bodies of the Supreme Soviet

The multiformity of the questions considered by the Supreme Soviet of the U.S.S.R., its organisation and forms of its activity make it necessary to have standing committees in the Soviet of the Union and the Soviet of Nationalities.

The standing committees are permanently acting auxiliary bodies of the chambers. Their tasks include preparation of conclusions on various questions and amendments to bills submitted for the consideration of the Supreme Soviet by the Government and other state bodies, mass organisations and deputies. Moreover, the functions of the committees include elaboration of bills on their own initiative or on the instructions of either chamber or the Presidium of the Supreme Soviet of the U.S.S.R. All the standing committees of the chambers enjoy equal rights in discharging their functions and exercise equal powers to legislate, i.e., their suggestions and remarks must without fail be considered by the appropriate chamber.

In exercising supreme control of the executive the Supreme Soviet of the U.S.S.R. also acts through the appropriate standing committees of the Soviet of the Union and the Soviet of Nationalities. The committees of the chambers control the observance of the Constitution of the U.S.S.R., the laws of the U.S.S.R. and other enactments of the Supreme Soviet and its Presidium by the ministries and departments of the U.S.S.R. and other state bodies and organisations.

The standing committees are, as a rule, formed during the first sessions of the chambers of each convocation and act as long as the chambers are in office, i.e., for four years. The committees are elected from among the deputies of the corresponding chambers. The character of the committees and their composition are determined by the chambers. The necessity for establishing standing committees arises from the laws in force. For example, Article 50 of the Constitution provides for organisation of Credentials Committees in the chambers; Article 32 provides for establishment of Legislative Proposals Committees; Regulations for these committees also envisage their formation.

Preliminary consideration and analysis of the national economic plan, budget and bills submitted to the Supreme Soviet, preparation of conclusions on them, initiative in elaborating bills, and control over the bodies accountable to the Supreme Soviet and its Presidium, all form an essential prerequisite for comprehensive and businesslike discussion and solution of problems which are under the jurisdiction of the highest representative body of state power of the U.S.S.R. Side by side with the Presidium of the Supreme Soviet the standing committees of the chambers ensure, both during the sessions and in the intervening periods, the continuity and effective activity of the Supreme Soviet.

The committees of the chambers play a very active role in solving the fundamental problems of the country's political life. Their growing activity is attested by the increasing number of deputies on these committees.

Committee	1st Convocation 1937-46		2nd Convocation 1946-50		3rd Convocation 1950-54		4th Convocation 1954-58		5th Convocation 1958-62		6th Convocation 1962-66	
	Soviet of the Union	Soviet of Nationalities	Soviet of the Union	Soviet of Nationalities	Soviet of the Union	Soviet of Nationalities	Soviet of the Union	Soviet of Nationalities	Soviet of the Union	Soviet of Nationalities	Soviet of the Union	Soviet of Nationalities
Credentials	11	11	15	15	17	17	17	17	21	21	21	21
Legislative Proposals	10	10	19	19	19	19	19	19	31	31	31	31
Budgetary (or Planning and Budgetary)	13	13	27	27	27	27	26	26	39	39	39	39
Foreign Relations	11	10	11	11	11	11	11	11	23	23	23	23
Economic (of the Soviet of Nationalities)	—	—	—	—	—	—	—	31	—	31	—	31

At the First Session of the Seventh Supreme Soviet of the U.S.S.R., held in August 1966, N. V. Podgorny suggested in his report that the number of standing committees be increased and that they be formed in accordance with the needs of the political, economic, social and cultural construction and with the various problems considered by the Supreme Soviet. At the same session the Soviet of the Union and the Soviet of Nationalities set up Planning and Budgetary, sectoral, Legislative Proposals, Foreign Affairs and Credentials Committees.

The formation of sectoral committees reflects a specialisation in the Supreme Soviet activity, particularly the necessity for a detailed study and careful analysis of the work of the various branches of the economy. The development of the committee system permits of a deeper analysis of the national economic plan and the budget not only on a country-wide or republican scale, but also within individual branches of the economy and concrete ministries; it also makes it possible to discover the reasons for shortcomings and the ways of eliminating them, as well as to increase the volume and improve the quality of production. The increased number of standing committees makes it also possible further to improve the law-making of the Supreme Soviet of the U.S.S.R.

The improved system of standing committees stimulates the all-round activities of the Supreme Soviet based on principles of managing the economy on a countrywide scale and of individual branches of the economy combined with an extension of the powers of the Union Republics and centralised planning.

The increase in the number of committees and in their membership (to 700) draws a large number of deputies into the permanent work of the Supreme Soviet.

Today the standing committees number 117 women. Among the committee members there are leaders of Party and government bodies, directors of industrial enterprises, chairmen of collective farms and rank-and-file collective farmers, workers—machine-builders, miners, oil workers, steel founders, weavers—trade union and Komsomol functionaries, writers and scientists. The committees are composed of representatives of some 50 nationalities inhabiting the Soviet Union.

Thus the standing committees are composed of representatives of all Union and Autonomous Republics, Autonomous Regions and National Areas. This makes possible the participation of deputies, who are familiar with the local peculiarities of the different areas of the country, in the elaboration and discussion of the national economic plans, the budget and the bills with due regard for these peculiarities in the laws and other enactments passed by the supreme representative body of the Soviet people. In formulating proposals on political, economic, social and cultural development the standing committees are guided by the interests of the U.S.S.R. as a whole and the interests of the Union Republics, the necessity for rational distribution of the productive forces, overall development and specialisation of the economies of the Union Republics, with due regard for the national and other peculiarities of the Union and Autonomous Republics, Autonomous Regions and National Areas.

The standing committees are accountable and responsible for all their activities to the chambers which elect them. The chambers guide the work of their committees; in between sessions the activities of all committees are co-ordinated and directed by the Presidium of the Supreme Soviet.

Each standing committee carries on its activity in a particular branch or a group of branches of the national economy and culture or in a certain sphere of work of the Supreme Soviet. The functions of the Presidium of the Supreme Soviet in co-ordinating the work of the committees assume particular importance in problems involving two or several committees. When necessary the Presidium refers bills to the committees for their conclusion or suggest which committees are to elaborate concrete problems and the ways in which these problems are to be tackled. For example, on July 27, 1959, the Presidium established in its decision that, since the Bill on the Budgetary Powers of the U.S.S.R. and the Union Republics touched upon questions in the competence of the Budgetary Committees of the chambers and the Economic Committee of the Soviet of Nationalities, it was necessary to refer this bill to these committees in order that their opinions may be taken into consideration when the bill is submitted for final consideration.

Very significant from this point of view was the Presidium's decision of December 20, 1966, which established the order of the work of the sectoral and other committees on bills prepared earlier by the Legislative Proposals Committees of the Soviet of the Union and the Soviet of Nationalities of the preceding convocation. It decreed, for example, that further work on the draft Fundamentals of Land Use will be carried on by eight committees: Committee for Agriculture, Committee for Industry, Transport and Communications, Committee for Construction and the Building Materials Industry, and Committees for Legislative Proposals. It is important to note that, whereas 62 members of the Legislative Proposals Committees worked on this bill before the organisation of sectoral committees, now this bill will be prepared by 228 members of the committees most interested in elaborating the basic principles of land use.

The meetings of the standing committees are called by their chairmen when necessary. For the meetings and for carrying out committee assignments the deputies are given leave from work with pay. The decisions of the committees are considered legal if their meetings are attended by at least two-thirds of their membership. All questions are decided by a simple majority vote. Members of the committees, who do not agree with the decision of the majority, have the right to speak in favour of their proposals at a sitting of a chamber or at a joint sitting of both chambers.

When preparing bills and conclusions, as well as when discharging control functions or considering other questions, the standing committees have the right to hear ministers, other representatives of the Government of the U.S.S.R. and the governments of the Republics, and leaders of all-Union and republican departments, send them appropriate recommendations, and demand that all bodies and offi cials submit the necessary materials pertaining to the question under the committee's consideration.

When necessary, the standing committees enlist the services of consultants from among scientists and specialists in particular branches of government. The meetings of the committees are attended with a consultative vote by deputies of the Supreme Soviet of the U.S.S.R., who are not members of the committees, and by representatives of the public and the press.

Legislative Proposals Committees

The tasks of the Legislative Proposals Committees of the chambers, each of which consists of 31 deputies, include elaboration of bills, as well as preliminary consideration and preparation of conclusions on bills of a general character submitted to the Supreme Soviet of the U.S.S.R. by other bodies, for example, on problems of the judicial system and judicial proceedings, civil, criminal and matrimonial law, etc. As a rule, the Legislative Proposals Committees submit to the chambers conclusions on all bills except those which are in the competence of other standing committees. When bills or conclusions are being prepared by sectoral committees the Legislative Proposals Committees may take part in their work by request of the corresponding sectoral committees or by instructions of either chamber or the Presidium of the Supreme Soviet of the U.S.S.R. By instructions of the Presidium of the Supreme Soviet or on their own initiative the committees also draft decrees which introduce changes into the law in force.

The work of the Legislative Proposals Committees is built on the principles of collegiate functioning, publicity and the help of the public.

The bills prepared or considered by the committees are carefully elaborated, checked or amended by special groups of deputies or by subcommittees. The membership of subcommittees (about 25-30 members, depending on the character of the problem) is approved by the respective committee. As a rule, in addition to deputies, the subcommittees include representatives of Party, trade union and other mass organisations, scientists, experts, representatives of ministries and departments. For example, the subcommittees of the Legislative Proposals Committees in the Sixth Supreme Soviet of the U.S.S.R., formed to elaborate the Fundamentals of Legislation on Exploitation of Water Resources, consisted of seven deputies representing various Union Republics, workers of the U.S.S.R. State Planning Committee, the All-Union Central Council of Trade Unions, the U.S.S.R. Ministry of Melioration and Water Economy, the U.S.S.R. Ministry of Power Development and Electrification, the U.S.S.R. Ministry of Fisheries, the U.S.S.R. Ministry of Public Health, the U.S.S.R. Ministry of the Merchant Marine, the U.S.S.R. Academy of Sciences, the All-Union Academy of Agriculture, Moscow State University, the All-Union Research Institute of Hydraulic Engineering and Melioration, and other organisations and departments. Such subcommittees are, as a rule, organised jointly by the respective committees of both chambers. However, each committee has the right to organise its own subcommittees. To elaborate problems jointly with sectoral committees, joint subcommittees or groups of deputies may also be set up.

The bills submitted by committees for conclusions, the proposals of deputy groups and subcommittees on such bills, as well as new bills, draft decrees and all necessary explanatory, reference and other materials appertaining to them are sent to all members of the committees localy. Each committee member enlists for consideration of a bill deputies of local Soviets, the services of specialists in the corresponding branches of the national economy and culture, representatives of mass organisations and scientists. Together with them the committee member studies the bill, analyses its contents with due regard for the peculiarities of the given Republic, geographical zone, etc. This method enables each committee member to collect and generalise, in the course of his work on a bill, the local experience, the requirements of the population of his constituency, all that is new and progressive and is born locally in the course of communist construction and needs consolidation by law.

An important factor in the work of the committees is the submittal of bills to Union Republics for conclusion. In order to reflect the practical experience of the Union Republics in the bills, the Legislative Proposals Committees solicit the opinion of the Presidiums of the Supreme Soviets of the Union Republics, standing committees and other republican bodies. For the same purpose the committee members and subcommittee experts go to Republics where they can acquaint themselves with the application of the law in force, and organise discussions of the bills in republican and local bodies, at industrial enterprises and in mass organisations. For competent conclusions on bills from the point of view of the latest achievements of science these bills are referred to scientific and research institutions. For example, the bills on the Fundamentals of Civil Legislation and the Fundamentals of Civil Procedure were sent for a conclusion to some 30 law faculties of universities and law institutes in Moscow and Union Republics.

The committees also draw upon the opinions, suggestions and remarks of individual citizens. For example, when preparing the conclusion on the State Pensions Bill, the committees studied more than 12,000 letters with suggestions for amending or supplementing the bill. Many of these suggestions were taken into consideration. Thousands of letters were read by the committees in connection with the preparation of the bills on the Fundamentals of Civil Legislation, Fundamentals of Civil Procedure, Fundamentals of Matrimonial Law, and other bills.

But the broad participation of the people in the discussions of the bills being prepared by the committees is ensured by their timely publication. For this purpose the Legislative Proposals Committees published the bills on the Fundamentals of Civil Legislation, the

Fundamentals of Civil Procedure, the Fundamentals of Criminal Legislation, etc., before submitting them to the Supreme Soviet.

The democratic methods and forms of work of the Legislative Proposals Committees help the Soviet law-maker take into account the collective experience of the masses and the achievements of science and practice, and see to it that the laws express most precisely the will and interests of the people, correctly regulate the economic, organisational, cultural and educational work, and contribute to the accomplishment of the tasks of communist construction and all-round development of the personality.

The Legislative Proposals Committees have of late become particularly active. They have elaborated important bills and draft decrees aimed at further improving socialist democracy, providing still greater opportunities for the Soviet people's participation in governing the state, extending the powers of the Union Republics, and improving the methods of state management of the economy and culture and the work of the state apparatus. Thus the committees prepared and submitted to the Supreme Soviet of the U.S.S.R. the Law on the Budgetary Powers of the U.S.S.R. and the Union Republics, the Law on the Order of Recalling Deputies to the Supreme Soviet of the U.S.S.R. (1959), etc.

The Supreme Soviet of the U.S.S.R. approved some important all-Union bills elaborated by the Legislative Proposals Committees and aimed at improving the Soviet judicial system, the civil and criminal legislation and judicial procedure and further strengthening socialist law and protection of the citizens' rights. The laws include the Law on Placing under the Jurisdiction of the Union Republics the Legislation on Their Judicial Systems and on the Passage of Civil, Criminal and Procedure Codes, the Statute of the Supreme Court of the U.S.S.R. (1957), the Fundamentals of Criminal Legislation of the U.S.S.R. and the Union Republics, the Fundamentals of Criminal Procedure of the U.S.S.R. and the Union Republics, the Fundamentals of Legislation on the Judicial System of the U.S.S.R., the Union and Autonomous Republics (1958), the Fundamentals of Civil Legislation of the U.S.S.R. and the Union Republics, the Fundamentals of Civil Procedure of the U.S.S.R. and the Union Republics (1961), etc.

Considerable work of preparing new bills is still being done by the Legislative Proposals Committees. They are elaborating new bills on the Fundamentals of Matrimonial Law and the Fundamentals of Corrective Labour Legislation. These committees are working together with the sectoral committees on new bills: Basic Principles of Land Use, Fundamentals of Legislation on Exploitation of Water Resources, Basic Principles of the Exploitation of Mineral Wealth, Basic Principles of Forest Exploitation, Fundamentals of Legislation on Health Protection, etc.

The Legislative Proposals Committees prepared conclusions and provided co-rapporteurs for the Supreme Soviet of the U.S.S.R. on a number of all-Union bills, such as the State Pensions and Pensions and Allowances for Collective Farmers.

The Bill on Pensions and Allowances for Collective Farmers submitted to the Supreme Soviet by the Central Committee of the Communist Party of the Soviet Union and the U.S.S.R. Council of Ministers in July 1964 was referred by the Presidium of the Supreme Soviet to the Legislative Proposals Committees for a conclusion. The committees took part in formulating this important law aimed at introducing a single and stable system of pensions for collective farmers.

Having examined this bill the committees suggested essential additions and amendments which were reported to a session of the Supreme Soviet. The suggestions included an amendment which sought to increase the number of members of the collective farmer's family entitled to a pension in the event of the loss of the bread-winner, to provide a 20 per cent increase in the pension, if the incapacity or death of the bread-winner was the result of a labour injury or occupational disease, and other amendments. The committees' suggestions were approved by the Supreme Soviet and were incorporated in the law.

On instructions of the Presidium of the Supreme Soviet of the U.S.S.R. the Legislative Proposals Committees prepare conclusions on draft decrees of a normative character. Thus in December 1964 the Soviet Government submitted to the Presidium of the Supreme Soviet of the U.S.S.R. a draft decree on the order of imposing fines for wasteful expenditure of electric power and heat. The Presidium referred this draft to the committees for a conclusion.

Considering the paramount economic importance of thrifty utilisation of the country's fuel and power resources and the fact that many industrial enterprises and organisations exceed their quotas of heat and electric power, the committees suggested that the officials guilty of such practices bear full responsibility. At the same time the committees proposed a number of amendments to the bill. In particular, in order to ensure the observance of the law and protect the citizens' rights the committees proposed to draw up a list of violations for which fines may be imposed and to enumerate officials responsible for such violations.

Attaching great importance to preventing neglect of duty, the committees suggested that the decree provide a possibility not only of imposing fines on those guilty of wasteful expenditure of power, but also of giving them warnings in cases where the character of the violation and the damage caused by them do not warrant a fine.

The draft decree proposed that the state electric power agencies be granted the right to impose fines without reference to Executive Committees of local Soviets. In order that the cases of wasteful expenditure of power may be considered more objectively and the educational significance of the administrative measures taken may be enhanced, the committees proposed that the decree contain a provision that the fines for wasteful expenditure of heat and electric power be imposed by administrative commissions of the local Soviets on representations made by authorised officials of the state agencies of electric power supervision.

The Presidium of the Supreme Soviet of the U.S.S.R. considered the conclusions made by the Legislative Proposals Committees, approved their amendments and issued the decree in the wording proposed by the committees.

According to established practice, in individual cases the Legislative Proposals Committees consider problems connected with republican legislation. Thus in 1960, in reply to requests received from Union Republics, the Legislative Proposals Committees made proposals aimed at uniforming the penalties provided in the codes of the Republics for certain grave crimes.

The tasks of the Legislative Proposals Committees also include control of the observance of the all-Union laws and decrees by bodies accountable to the Supreme Soviet and its Presidium for questions pertaining to the terms of reference of these committees, and cooperation in implementing the Supreme Soviet decisions. The committees hear reports made by heads of ministries and departments, expose the shortcomings in their activities and elaborate recommendations aimed at eliminating these shortcomings.

In December 1963 the Legislative Proposals Committees considered the question of observance of the laws which regulate the state registration of all land and the utilisation of the country's farm land. The consideration of this question at a joint meeting of the committees was preceded by preparatory work in a specially formed subcommittee and in various localities. A group of deputies and experts familiarised themselves on state and collective farms and in local Soviets with the organisation of land registration, proper utilisation of land, soil improvement, control of erosion and other harmful soil processes. The services of the Institute of Agricultural Economies, the Dokuchayev Soil Institute, other institutions and individual scientists and experts were enlisted in the work of preparing the question.

The committees heard the report of the subcommittee and the communications of representatives of the U.S.S.R. State Planning Committee, ministries of the Ukrainian S.S.R. and Kirghiz S.S.R., and the Executive Committees of the Stavropol Territory and Saratov Regional Soviets.

Noting a certain improvement in the utilisation of farm lands and land registration the committees pointed out the essential shortcomings, namely, the failure of a number of regions to draw up soil maps, which hindered the organisation of intensive agricultural production, specialisation of the farms and the effective use of mineral and other fertiliser; inadequate study of the economic effect of agricultural land and the slow work of introducing a land cadastre; poor control of water and wind erosion in some areas, owing to which agricultural crops and arable land have decreased.

Broad discussions of the foregoing questions by the committees attended by heads of ministries and departments of the U.S.S.R. and individual Union Republics, agricultural specialists, economists and lawyers, as well as the materials furnished by local check-ups, enabled the committees to make proposals for improving land utilisation and registration, and to submit a detailed report to the Government. Appropriate bodies were instructed to carry out a number of measures aimed at rational utilisation of the country's farm lands.

By way of controlling the executive the Legislative Proposals Committees also considered other questions, for example, the functioning of corrective labour institutions and the occupations of the inmates, and the observance of the Law on Universal and Compulsory Eight-Year Schooling in the R.S.F.S.R., the Azerbaijan S.S.R. and the Kirghiz S.S.R. The committees' proposals on the latter question were considered by the Presidium of the Supreme Soviet of the U.S.S.R. and concrete decisions were taken, for example, provision of free railway and other transportation for schoolchildren living in rural areas.

Early in 1965 the committees checked on the observance of the Law on Pensions and Allowances for Collective Farmers. The committee members studied the collective farmers' social security in a number of Republics and regions, and in December, at a joint meeting of the committees of both chambers, heard reports of the Ministers of Social Security of the R.S.F.S.R., the Azerbaijan S.S.R. and the Turkmen S.S.R. and adopted appropriate recommendations.

Planning and Budgetary Committees

The Soviet of the Union and the Soviet of Nationalities of the Supreme Soviet of the U.S.S.R. of six convocations formed budgetary committees (27 to 39 deputies each) for a preliminary consideration of the State Budget of the U.S.S.R. and a report on the financial results for the preceding year. In view of the fact that since 1957 these committees annually considered and gave their conclusions to the chambers not only on the State Budget, but also on the national economic plan, the First Session of the Seventh Supreme Soviet of the U.S.S.R., held in 1966, reorganised these committees into Planning and Budgetary Committees both in the Soviet of the Union and the Soviet of Nationalities. These committees are now doing the work previously done by the Budgetary Committees.

The Planning and Budgetary Committees consist of deputies from all the Union and most Autonomous Republics. The members of the committees are foremost workers and collective farmers, managers of industrial enterprises and state farms, leaders of republican and local Party and government bodies, workers of public education and

Joint meeting of the Planning and Budgetary Committee and the sectoral committees of the Soviet of the Union chaired by Deputy P. Rozenko. Deputy Lomonosov is speaking

the health services, and scientists; the committees also draw upon the knowledge and experience of other workers, consult experts and together with them analyse the submitted materials, check up on the calculations and consider the proposals received from different parts of the country.

The tasks of the Planning and Budgetary Committees include preliminary study of the long-term and annual plans for the development of the economy and the State Budget of the U.S.S.R. submitted by the Soviet Government for the consideration of the Soviet Parliament.

The committees also consider the annual reports of the Soviet Government on the execution of the State Budget of the U.S.S.R. and thereby exercise control over the revenues and expenditures and over the observance of financial regulations.

The tasks of the committees also include elaboration or preliminary consideration of all-Union bills on planning the national economy, budget and finances, submitted to the Supreme Soviet of the U.S.S.R. for approval.

The Planning and Budgetary Committees, like the other standing committees of the Soviet Parliament, exercise systematic control over the activities of the ministries and departments and help in the implementation of the decisions taken by the Supreme Soviet of the U.S.S.R.

The Planning and Budgetary Committees convene when necessary. They consider the economic plan and State Budget of the U.S.S.R. for the coming year and the report on the execution of the budget for the preceding year. The work of the committees usually starts a month or a month and a half before the session of the Supreme Soviet.

The Planning and Budgetary Committees study the plan and budget in close contact with the sectoral standing committees of the chambers. When necessary, for consideration of different parts of the plan and budget, the committees form joint subcommittees or groups and establish other forms of co-operation. The Planning and Budgetary Committees of both chambers meet together to hear a report of the Chairman of the State Planning Committee on the state plan for the development of the economy of the U.S.S.R. for the coming year and a report of the Minister of Finance of the U.S.S.R. on the State Budget of the U.S.S.R. for the coming year and on the financial results for the preceding year. On the instructions of the Soviet Government the rapporteurs describe in detail and substantiate the draft plan and draft budget submitted to the Supreme Soviet of the U.S.S.R. for approval.

In considering the plan and budget for 1967 each Planning and Budgetary Committee and all the sectoral committees formed about 15 joint groups of deputies for a detailed study of the different parts of the plan and budget, including the basic (summary) indices of the national economic plan, the basic items of the State Budget, the revenues, the heavy industry, the food industry, trade, everyday services and the light industry, agriculture, transport and communications, construction and the building materials industry, public education, science and culture, health and social security, the report on financial results, and the draft plans and draft budgets of the Union Republics (three groups of deputies).

The subcommittees or groups of deputies enlist the services of consultants—experts on different branches of the national economy and on budgetary and financial problems—workers of the U.S.S.R. State Planning Committee, the U.S.S.R. State Building Committee, the U.S.S.R. Ministry of Finance, the U.S.S.R. Central Statistical Board, the U.S.S.R. State Bank, the U.S.S.R. Bank for Construction and other ministries and departments. More than 200 consultants take part in the work of the committees and their subcommittees.

The work of the subcommittees is done according to a plan drawn up beforehand and lasts two or three weeks. Each subcommittee hears reports and explanations by representatives of the U.S.S.R. State Planning Committee, the U.S.S.R. Ministry of Finance and other ministries and departments, as well as representatives of the Councils of Ministers of the Union Republics, receives and analyses the statistical materials, checks on the correctness of the drafts and calculations of the different parts of the plan, revenues and expenditures. In some cases the subcommittees summon to their sittings managers of industrial enterprises, building organisations, educational institutions, public health services, scientific and designing organisations, hear their reports and receive from them materials and explanations on questions of interest to the subcommittees.

The work of the Planning and Budgetary Committees on the drafts of the natonal economic plan and the State Budget is published in the press, which enables people to submit their proposals. The proposals are submitted by workers of different branches of the economy, culture, science and the arts, as well as by individual heads of industrial enterprises and organisations, and are concerned mainly with rationalisation of the production processes, different branches of the national economy, improvement of the state apparatus and avoidance of superfluous expenditures. All these proposals are given consideration by the committees or their subcommittees; sometimes they are referred to ministries and departments for consideration and action with due control of the ensuing results.

The conclusions and proposals of the subcommittees or groups of deputies are considered at plenary meetings of the Planning and Budgetary Committees to which heads of the U.S.S.R. State Planning Committee, the U.S.S.R. Ministry of Finance and other Union ministries and departments are invited; officially authorised representatives of the Councils of Ministers of the Union Republics also attend the meetings at which the plans and budgets of the Union Republics are discussed.

The Planning and Budgetary Committees also consider the proposals and applications of the Councils of Ministers of the Union Republics, and the ministries and departments of the U.S.S.R. for changes in the various indices of the national economic plan, changes in the correlation between the revenues and expenditures envisaged in the drafts of the plan and budget of the different Republics, ministries and departments.

After considering all the materials the Planning and Budgetary Committees, independently or jointly with the sectoral committees, submit to the corresponding chamber their conclusions on the national economic plan, the State Budget and the report on its execution.

The conclusions on the plan and budget for 1967, as well as on the report on the financial results for 1965, were prepared and submitted to the chambers jointly by the Planning and Budgetary Committees and the sectoral committees on industry, transport and communications, construction and building materials industry, agriculture, public health and social security, public education, science and culture, trade and everyday services. The conclusions are sent in due time to deputies in order that they may have enough time to prepare for the debate on these questions in the Supreme Soviet.

The conclusions of the Planning and Budgetary Committees and the sectoral committees contain a general evaluation of the drafts of the plan and the budget and of the report on the financial results, proposals for amendments to the plan and budget considered desirable by the committees, critical remarks on the work of ministries, departments, planning and financial bodies, and recommendations for eliminating the shortcomings observed in their work by the committees.

During the debate on the national economic plan and State Budget for 1967 in the Soviet Parliament the Planning and Budgetary Committees and the sectoral committees made joint reports on these questions at the sittings of the corresponding chambers. On the committees' instructions reports were made by the chairmen of the Planning and Budgetary Committees.

These committees also refer to the ministries and departments of the U.S.S.R. and the Councils of Ministers of the Union Republics extracts from the decisions of the committees and the reports of the subcommittees on different questions which were not duly reflected in the conclusions and co-reports of the committees at the session of the Supreme Soviet of the U.S.S.R.

The Planning and Budgetary Committees make proposals on amendments to the annual economic plan and State Budget submitted to the Supreme Soviet of the U.S.S.R. for approval. After the debates on the plans and budgets for 1963, 1964, 1965 and 1966 the Sixth Supreme Soviet increased the revenues, on the proposals of the Budgetary Committees, by 480.7 million rubles. It accepted the proposals of the Planning and Budgetary Committees and the sectoral committees to increase the 1967 revenues by 120 million rubles. These sums of additionally revealed financial resources were used to augment the allocations to the budgets of the Union Republics for capital repairs of buildings, housing social and cultural institutions, improvement of town planning, public services and amenities, etc. The Supreme Soviet also approved the committees' proposals to increase the output and sales of many consumer goods.

Besides the direct amendments to the plan and budget the committees submit important proposals on various aspects of the development of the economy of the U.S.S.R. and the Union Republics, their elaboration and realisation requiring a longer time and additional financial and material resources.

The proposals of the Planning and Budgetary Committees on the plan and budget are carried into effect as follows: on some problems the State Planning Committee, ministries and departments of the U.S.S.R. work out measures which will be submitted to the Government for consideration, while some proposals are referred to the central planning bodies which draw up long-term plans for the development of the Soviet economy.

Thus, for example, in considering the plan and budget for 1965 the Budgetary Committee of the Soviet of the Union devoted serious attention to providing the national economy, especially the municipal services, with fuel. A study of this question showed that despite certain difficulties in providing the economy with fuel the plans for putting coal mines into operation were not fulfilled. The coal industry was not fully provided with capital investments and up-to-date machinery, while specialised building organisations of this industry were working for other industries.

The Budgetary Committee submitted a proposal to increase the coal-mining capacities, improve the designing of coal mines on the basis of modern technology, continue to re-equip the coal mines in operation and boost the output of coal, peat and other local fuel.

In accordance with the proposals of the Budgetary Committee the assignment for coal-mining and gas-extraction was increased in 1965. Measures were taken to ensure the additional output of fuel and to supply the fuel industry with the necessary equipment and materials. Proposals were made to enhance the material incentives for the miners.

Extensive measures were taken to materialise the proposals of the Planning and Budgetary Committees and the sectoral committees to find possibilities for additional production of consumer goods and to improve their quality.

Several decisions of the U.S.S.R. Council of Ministers changing the existing system of planning and the material encouragement of workers were adopted to enhance the incentives of the enterprises, to boost production, extend the assortment and improve the quality of consumer goods.

In considering the economic plan and the State Budget of the U.S.S.R. for 1967 the Planning and Budgetary Committees and the sectoral committees devoted serious attention to the new system of planning and economic stimulation. In their co-reports to the Supreme Soviet the committees noted that the economic reform now in progress in the light, food and certain other industries required that greater deductions from the profits be made in 1967 for the material encouragement funds in industry, that the enterprises be provided with more materials and equipment, that new wholesale prices be introduced in all industries at specified periods and that the economic planning be improved.

Attaching paramount importance to the economic reform, the U.S.S.R. Council of Ministers instructed appropriate organisations to make a special study of all the remarks and proposals of the committees and to take decisions on them, prepare and submit proposals on questions, which are in the competence of the Government, to the Council of Ministers for consideration.

The committees found that one of the serious shortcomings in capital construction was the extremely inadequate utilisation of local building materials. In many areas too little attention is devoted to the production of building materials despite the abundance of raw materials. For this reason the committees recommended that the State Planning Committee be instructed to provide in the plans for the subsequent years capital investments for the development of the building materials industry and the construction industry in order to supply the construction jobs with all the necessary building materials and elements.

The committees have now become much more active and their control functions have increased. In addition to considering the drafts of the national economic plan and the State Budget, as well as the annual reports on their fulfilment, the committees also exercise control over the fulfilment of the plan and the financial results all the year round. At a joint meeting in July 1964 the Budgetary Committees heard a report on and discussed the question of the fulfilment of the plan and of the financial results for the first six months of 1964. During the debates on the aforesaid questions the members of the Budgetary Committees noted that, despite the successful fulfilment of the plan and the good financial results in 1964 for the U.S.S.R. as a whole, there were essential shortcomings in the work of various state committees, ministries, industrial enterprises and building organisations, namely, the internal reserves were not as yet sufficiently tapped for increasing the output and improving the quality of the production.

Representatives of the U.S.S.R. State Planning Committee, other state committees, ministries of the U.S.S.R. and Councils of Ministers of Union Republics took part in the discussions of the questions under consideration. The parliamentary committees passed a resolution aimed at ensuring the fulfilment of the national economic plan and the State Budget in 1964, making up for the lag in the output of certain enterprises during the first six months of the year, putting into operation the industrial enterprises which were under construction and failed to be commissioned during the first six months, and more completely utilising the reserves available in industry and construction.

The resolution of the Budgetary Committees was referred to the Council of Ministers. The latter instructed the U.S.S.R. State Planning Committee, the State Building Committee, the state sectoral and production committees, the ministries and departments of the U.S.S.R. and the Councils of Ministers of the Union Republics to consider the recommendations of the Budgetary Committees, take the necessary measures and report on the results to the Council of Ministers and the Budgetary Committees.

The proposals and recommendations of the Budgetary Committees concerning individual Republics, ministries and departments were considered by the Councils of Ministers of the Republics, the boards of ministries, committees or chief administrations; resolutions were passed on them, orders and instructions were issued, and control over their translation into reality was established.

The consideration of the aforesaid questions in the committees greatly helped to fulfil the national economic plan and execute the State Budget in 1964.

Sectoral Committees

The First Session of the Seventh Supreme Soviet of the U.S.S.R. (August 1966) has gone down in the history of Soviet democracy as an important event. As was already stated, acting on the report of N. V. Podgorny, President of the Presidium of the Supreme Soviet of the U.S.S.R., the chambers passed decisions to organise new standing committees and to increase the membership of the existing committees.

In passing this decision the Supreme Soviet was guided by Lenin's well-known advice to the effect that the deputies "themselves should decide, themselves should observe their laws, themselves should check up on what happens in life and themselves should be directly accountable to their electors". The deputies of the Soviets are at once authorised representatives and executors of the people's will. That is why they do not break with production and are well aware of the needs of their electors and of the country at large. This enables the elected representatives of the people to find correct solutions of complex state problems.

And the number of such problems grows with each passing year. Industrial and agricultural production is continuously expanding, new branches of industry are appearing, science is making important discoveries, the material and cultural requirements are increasing.

The Soviet Parliament has to deal ever more concretely with problems of economy, culture and the people's welfare. Because of this the Soviet of the Union and the Soviet of Nationalities set up six standing sectoral committees each, namely, Committees for Industry, Transport and Communications, for Construction and Building Materials Industry, for Agriculture, for Health and Social Security, for Public Education, Science and Culture, and for Trade and Public Amenities. These committees number a total of 412 deputies.

It is but natural that the formation of the Planning and Budgetary Committees and sectoral committees to deal with problems of economy and culture obviated the necessity of having the Economic Committee of the Soviet of Nationalities, and the latter was abolished.

The sectoral committees are in a position more concretely and with good knowledge to study the state of and the prospects for the development of the economy and culture on a countrywide scale or in an individual Republic, more deeply to analyse the work of ministries and departments and to reveal the reasons for the existing shortcomings. Favourable conditions are being set up for successful control of the observance of the laws and enactments passed by the Supreme Soviet of the U.S.S.R. and its Presidium, as well as for drafting new laws, decisions and decrees submitted to the Supreme Soviet for approval.

The first serious step in the work of the newly organised committees was consideration of the state plan for the development of the

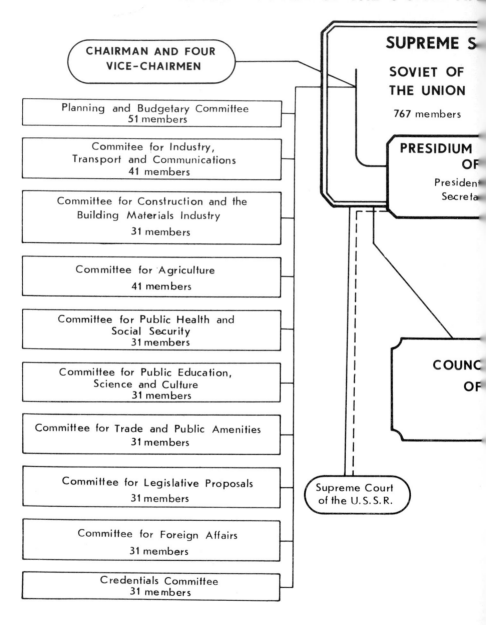

CHAIRMAN AND FOUR
VICE-CHAIRMEN

Planning and Budgetary Committee
51 members

Commitee for Industry,
Transport and Communications
41 members

Committee for Construction and the
Building Materials Industry
31 members

Committee for Agriculture
41 members

Committee for Public Health and
Social Security
31 members

Committee for Public Education,
Science and Culture
31 members

Committee for Trade and Public Amenities
31 members

Committee for Legislative Proposals
31 members

Committee for Foreign Affairs
31 members

Credentials Committee
31 members

SUPREME S

SOVIET OF
THE UNION

767 members

PRESIDIUM
OF
President
Secreta

COUNC
OF

Supreme Court
of the U.S.S.R.

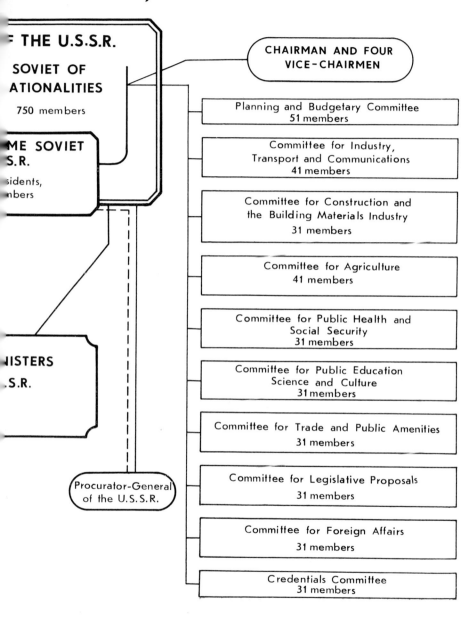

THE U.S.S.R.

SOVIET OF
ATIONALITIES

750 members

ME SOVIET
S.R.

sidents,
nbers

IISTERS
S.R.

Procurator-General
of the U.S.S.R.

CHAIRMAN AND FOUR
VICE-CHAIRMEN

Planning and Budgetary Committee
51 members

Committee for Industry,
Transport and Communications
41 members

Committee for Construction and
the Building Materials Industry
31 members

Committee for Agriculture
41 members

Committee for Public Health and
Social Security
31 members

Committee for Public Education
Science and Culture
31 members

Committee for Trade and Public Amenities
31 members

Committee for Legislative Proposals
31 members

Committee for Foreign Affairs
31 members

Credentials Committee
31 members

national economy and of the State Budget for 1967. They combined efforts with the Planning and Budgetary Committees. Each chamber organised groups of deputies which included members of the sectoral committees and those of the Planning and Budgetary Committees. As a rule, these groups are headed by the chairmen of the sectoral committees.

Upon finishing the consideration of the country's plan and budget the groups reported their proposals and remarks to the Planning and Budgetary Committees of the chambers. Their proposals were accepted and included in the general findings of the committees considering the 1967 plan for the development of the national economy and the state budget of the U.S.S.R.

The plenary meetings of the sectoral committees held later, heard the reports of their representatives in the groups dealing with the plan and budget and approved their work. Of some questions not included in the general conclusion of the committees the sectoral committees decided to submit their proposals directly to the relevant ministries and departments of the U.S.S.R. For example, the Committee of the Soviet of the Union for Construction and the Building Materials Industry addressed a letter to the U.S.S.R. State Planning Committee recommending that the latter take measures to provide capital construction with materials and equipment. Letters suggesting measures to hasten the development of the building materials industry were referred by the Committee to the U.S.S.R. State Building Committee and the U.S.S.R. Bank for Construction.

The Committee for Public Health and Social Security of the Soviet of the Union referred to the U.S.S.R. Ministry of Public Health a letter on the necessity of eliminating the existing shortcomings in the hospital treatment of the population. The U.S.S.R. Ministry of Finance and the All-Union Central Council of Trade Unions were sent letters on the need to alter the section of the law on social insurance which deals with paying for sick leave and for care of children under 3 years of age for the duration of their illness.

In December 1966 the Presidium of the Supreme Soviet of the U.S.S.R. instructed the Legislative Proposals Committees, jointly with the sectoral committees, to continue their work on the bills which were elaborated by the Legislative Proposals Committees of the Sixth Supreme Soviet. In this connection the sectoral committees of the chambers formed joint working bodies for each bill.

All the sectoral committees check up on the observance of the law governing the 1967 economic plan and the State Budget, and the realisation of the proposals made by the committees during the examination of the plan and budget. The ministries and departments of the U.S.S.R., as well as the Councils of Ministers of the Union Republics, inform the committees of the measures they take to ensure the observance of the laws on the plan and budget, approved by the Supreme Soviet of the U.S.S.R. and on the proposals of the sectoral committees. The formation of sectoral committees has set up favourable conditions for deeper preliminary consideration of the questions of the national economy and culture and has made it possible to enlist for the preparation of documents on these questions the services of a large number of deputies working in industry, agriculture, science, culture and other spheres. This guarantees a competent consideration and submittal of proposals with due regard for the local experience and interests of each Union Republic and the entire unity of nations of the Union of Soviet Socialist Republics.

Foreign Affairs Committees

The terms of reference of the Foreign Affairs Committees of the Soviet of the Union and the Soviet of Nationalities include:

submittal to the chambers of the Supreme Soviet of conclusions on bills concerned with foreign relations and referred to the Supreme Soviet of the U.S.S.R. for approval;

preparation on their own initiative and submittal of bills and other Soviet foreign policy acts to the Supreme Soviet of the U.S.S.R. or one of its chambers for consideration;

submittal to the Supreme Soviet of the U.S.S.R. or its Presidium of conclusions on ratification, denunciation or annulment of the most

Joint meeting of the Committees for Foreign Affairs of the two chambers of the Soviet Parliament

important treaties, conventions and agreements concluded by the Soviet Union with foreign countries.

The Foreign Affairs Committees have the right to hear at their sittings representatives of the Government of the U.S.S.R., the Ministry of Foreign Affairs, representatives of other ministries and departments, and to demand the relevant materials from various institutions and organisations.

During the term of office of the Supreme Soviet in 1950-1967 the Foreign Affairs Committees considered many urgent international issues and submitted their proposals and recommendations on them to the Soviet Parliament.

In February 1955 the committees prepared a draft Declaration of the Supreme Soviet of the U.S.S.R. to Establish and Develop Inter-Parliamentary Relations. The Declaration was adopted by the Fourth Supreme Soviet.

On December 25, 1958, the Foreign Affairs Committees produced at a joint session a draft resolution to the Supreme Soviet of the U.S.S.R. on ceasing the tests of atomic and hydrogen weapons and on the Berlin question. This resolution was unanimously adopted by the Fifth Supreme Soviet.

In October 1959 the committees elaborated a draft Appeal of the Fifth Supreme Soviet of the U.S.S.R. to the Parliaments of All Countries on General and Complete Disarmament. The Supreme Soviet adopted this Appeal.

In January 1960, after the passage of the Law on a New Considerable Reduction in the Armed Forces of the U.S.S.R., the Fifth Supreme Soviet of the U.S.S.R. adopted, on the proposal of the Foreign Affairs Committees, an Appeal to the Parliaments and Governments of All Countries to follow the example of the Soviet Union and take practical measures on their part to reduce their armed forces. Regrettably, this proposal, like many other Soviet proposals aimed at strengthening the peace among peoples, was not countenanced by the parliaments of the capitalist countries.

In April 1962 the Foreign Affairs Committees of the Sixth Supreme Soviet examined the main points of the report of the U.S.S.R. Minister of Foreign Affairs on the Geneva talks made by him at the First Session of the Sixth Supreme Soviet and decided to recommend to the Supreme Soviet that it approve the foreign policy of the Soviet Government. The Supreme Soviet passed a resolution approving the Soviet foreign policy.

On August 3, 1966, the Sixth Supreme Soviet, on the initiative of the Foreign Affairs Committees, adopted a Declaration of the Supreme Soviet of the Union of Soviet Socialist Republics on the Intensification of Aggression by American Imperialism in Vietnam.

A large part of the work of the Foreign Affairs Committees consists in preparing conclusions and recommendations for the Presidium of the Supreme Soviet on ratifying the most important treaties, conventions and agreements concluded by the Soviet Union with foreign countries.

In recent years the Foreign Affairs Committees have recommended the Presidium of the Supreme Soviet to ratify:

the trade agreement between the U.S.S.R. and the Iraqi Republic and the protocol on Soviet trade delegation in the Iraqi Republic (December 1958);

the agreement on economic and technical aid to be rendered by the Soviet Union to the United Arab Republic in building the first section of the Aswan High Dam (February 1959);

the agreement between the Government of the U.S.S.R. and the Government of the Argentine Republic on credit deliveries of machinery from the U.S.S.R. to Argentina for her oil industry (February 1959);

the treaty on the Antarctic (October 1960);

the convention on territorial waters and the adjacent zone, on the high seas and on the continental shelf (October 1960);

the treaty on the regime on the Soviet-Rumanian state border, co-operation and mutual assistance in border questions (June 1961).

To discuss the most important treaties and agreements the Foreign Affairs Committees assemble at joint sittings.

On August 29, 1961, they considered the proposal of the Council of Ministers, referred to them by the Presidium of the Supreme Soviet, to ratify the Treaty of Friendship, Co-operation and Mutual Assistance between the U.S.S.R. and the Korean People's Democratic Republic signed in Moscow on July 6, 1961. By their recommendation the Presidium of the Supreme Soviet ratified this treaty.

On August 31, 1963, the Foreign Affairs Committees jointly considered the proposal for ratifying the Treaty on Banning Nuclear Tests in the Atmosphere, Outer Space and Under Water, signed in Moscow on behalf of the governments of the U.S.S.R., Great Britain and the U.S.A. on August 5, 1963.

After a discussion the committees approved the proposal of the Council of Ministers to ratify the treaty and recommended its ratification to the Presidium of the Supreme Soviet of the U.S.S.R.

On September 24, 1964, the Foreign Affairs Committees examined at their joint session the proposal of the Council of Ministers, referred to them for a conclusion, to ratify the Treaty of Friendship, Mutual Assistance and Co-operation between the Soviet Union and the German Democratic Republic, concluded in Moscow on June 12, 1964.

The deputies speaking at the sittings described the treaty as a document that fully corresponded to the interests of the Soviet Union and the German Democratic Republic, the interests of all nations struggling for peace and security. The members of the committees unanimously approved the treaty and decided to recommend it to the Presidium of the Supreme Soviet of the U.S.S.R. for ratification.

On April 14, 1965, the Foreign Affairs Committees studied the proposal of the Council of Ministers to ratify the Treaty of Friendship, Co-operation and Mutual Assistance between the Soviet Union and the Polish People's Republic, signed in Warsaw on April 8, 1965. Approving the proposal of the Council of Ministers, the committees recommended the treaty to the Presidium of the Supreme Soviet of the U.S.S.R. for ratification.

On September 2, 1965, the committees considered a protocol on prolonging the term of the Neutrality and Non-Aggression Pact between the U.S.S.R. and Afghanistan, concluded on June 24, 1931, and the Soviet-Yugoslav agreement on economic and technical aid in the construction by Yugoslavia of a hydropower and shipping system on the Danube, signed in Moscow in March 1965.

By recommendation of the committees the foregoing documents were ratified by the Presidium of the Supreme Soviet.

On February 9, 1966, the Foreign Affairs Committees passed at their joint session a resolution to recommend the Presidium of the Supreme Soviet to ratify the Treaty of Friendship, Co-operation and Mutual Assistance between the Soviet Union and the Mongolian People's Republic, signed in Ulan Bator on January 15, 1966. At the same sitting the Committees also recommended the Presidium of the Supreme Soviet to ratify the agreement on cultural and scientific co-operation between the U.S.S.R. and Pakistan signed in Rawalpindi on June 5, 1965.

The joint sessions of the Foreign Affairs Committees were reported in the Soviet press and evoked a broad response in the foreign press.

The Foreign Affairs Committees often meet with foreign parliamentarians. The committee members travel abroad with Supreme Soviet delegations. Several delegations were headed on such journeys by members of the Foreign Affairs Committees. Moreover, the committee members give interviews to foreign parliamentary delegations.

Thus, a meeting of the Turkish Parliamentary Delegation and the Foreign Affairs Committees of both chambers of the Supreme Soviet was organised in June 1963.

At this meeting committee members gave the guests a detailed account of the foreign policy principles of the Soviet Union, the work of the Foreign Affairs Committees and the principles of economic relations of the Soviet Union with other countries. After the meeting the Turkish parliamentarians noted that it had enabled them to gain a better understanding of Soviet foreign policy and that they were persuaded that the supreme body of the Soviet state devotes much attention to this problem.

On September 15, 1966, the Foreign Affairs Committees met in the Kremlin with a delegation of the Foreign Relations Committee of the French National Assembly travelling over the Soviet Union.

The deputies of the Supreme Soviet and the French parliamentarians discussed the problems of interest to both countries, including the most important international issues, namely, European security, the German problem, the ban on atomic weapons, universal disarmament, the Vietnam question, etc. According to the members of the meeting, such an exchange of opinions helps to draw the points of view nearer and improve the bilateral relations.

The work of the Foreign Affairs Committees is very helpful in the successful pursuit of Soviet foreign policy and in strengthening peace throughout the world.

By actively participating in Soviet foreign policy the members of the Foreign Affairs Committees express not only their opinion, but also the will of the millions of their electors. This is manifested in the day-to-day work of the committee members, their speeches in the Supreme Soviet of the U.S.S.R. and the questions they put to the Government of the U.S.S.R. and the ministers. Questions on Soviet foreign policy or various international problems were addressed to the Government on behalf of a group of deputies, including the members of the Foreign Affairs Committees, at the sessions of the Supreme Soviet of the U.S.S.R. in June 1956, October 1957, December 1965, etc.

Credentials Committees

The Credentials Committees, like all other standing committees, are elected by each chamber for the same term as the Supreme Soviet. According to the Constitution of the U.S.S.R. their terms of reference include checking up on the credentials of the deputies of the corresponding chambers. Upon representation of the Credentials Committees the chambers may either recognise the credentials or annul the elections of individual deputies. Annulment of the elections, i.e., their invalidation, may take place in cases where the violations of the Constitution of the U.S.S.R. or of the Regulations for Election to the Supreme Soviet of the U.S.S.R. were such as to cast doubts on the correctness of their returns. The chambers of the Supreme Soviet of the U.S.S.R. have never had a case of annulling elections in any constituency because the requirements of the Constitution of the U.S.S.R. and the Electoral Law have always been strictly observed. At the First Session of the Seventh Supreme Soviet of the U.S.S.R. the chambers approved, after the reports of the Credentials Committees, the credentials of all the 767 deputies of the Soviet of the Union and all the 750 deputies of the Soviet of Nationalities elected to the Supreme Soviet of the U.S.S.R. on June 12, 1966.

When a seat in the Supreme Soviet of the U.S.S.R. is rendered vacant before the expiry of the term of the Supreme Soviet, new elections are held in the corresponding constituency. The check-up on the correctness of the credentials of the deputies elected in place of those whose seats have been vacated is also made by the Credentials Committees. These committees report the results of their check-up to the corresponding chamber.

The Credentials Committees of the Soviet of the Union and the Soviet of Nationalities were elected at the First Session of the Seventh Supreme Soviet. Each committee consists of a chairman and 30 members.

Ad Hoc Committees

In addition to the standing committees set up by the chambers the Supreme Soviet may, for separate tasks, form ad hoc committees. These are, for example, committees for drafting laws, editorial committees, etc. The Constitution envisages that the Supreme Soviet may, when it deems it necessary, appoint inquiry and auditing committees on any occasion.

In July 1964, pending the approval of the Law on Pensions and Allowances for Collective Farmers the Supreme Soviet of the U.S.S.R. set up an ad hoc committee to draw up proposals for deductions from the collective-farm incomes and the way these deductions were to be transferred to the centralised all-Union fund for collective farmers' social security. This committee numbered 52 deputies—collective-farm chairmen, collective farmers, agricultural specialists, Party and government representatives. The committee considered the participation of collective farms in forming the centralised fund and the organisational measures required to carry the Law on Pensions and Allowances to Collective Farmers into effect.

The committee studied the proposals of the deputies on these questions made in the Supreme Soviet, as well as the letters and proposals the committee received from citizens, materials of the U.S.S.R. State Planning Committee, the Central Statistical Board of the U.S.S.R., the U.S.S.R. Ministry of Finance, and other all-Union and republican departments. To make a careful study of the questions, particularly of the records of the farmers' participation in collective production and the records of the economic activities of the collective farms, the committee formed a subcommittee of experts, scientific workers, representatives of the State Planning Committee, the Ministry of Finance, the Ministry of Agriculture, the Central Statistical Board and other ministries and departments. The members of the committee and subcommittee enlisted the services of specialists from appropriate all-Union and republican departments and scientific workers and together with them visited many Union Republics for a random study of the collective farms. Appropriate research institutes were instructed to prepare conclusions on the methods of making deductions from the collective-farm incomes for the centralised collective farmers' social security fund. The services of a wide range of specialists and scientists were enlisted to help in this work.

The committee submitted its proposals on the aforesaid questions to the Council of Ministers. In accordance with them the Soviet Government passed a decision on the amount of the deductions to be made from the collective-farm incomes, the methods of making these deductions for the centralised all-Union collective farmers' social security fund and the organisational measures to carry this law into effect; it also approved the rules for granting and paying pensions to collective farmers, for granting and paying maternity allowances to collective-farm women, for the centralised collective farmers' social security fund, collective farmers' social security councils and committees for granting pensions and allowances to collective farmers.

In October 1965 the Supreme Soviet of the U.S.S.R. discussed, on the motion of the Council of Ministers, the question of improving the management of industry.

In connection with the consideration of this question the Government submitted to the Supreme Soviet a bill on Changes in the System of Industrial Management and Reorganisation of a Number of Government Bodies, prepared on the basis of the decisions of the September (1965) Plenary Meeting of the Central Committee of the Communist Party of the Soviet Union. For a preliminary examination of this bill with due regard for the proposals of the deputies, the Supreme Soviet formed an ad hoc committee of 25 deputies of the Soviet of the Union and 25 deputies of the Soviet of Nationalities.

During the debates on the question of improving the management of industry at the Supreme Soviet session deputies submitted a number of proposals aimed at eliminating the shortcomings in industrial management and improving the forms and methods of administration; they also made suggestions on measures planned in the Republics and individual localities to improve the management of industry.

The proposals and remarks made by the deputies were studied at the sittings of the chambers; when the debates ended the committee had a plenary meeting at which the bill was considered and all the remarks and proposals of the deputies were analysed.

The committee decided to approve the bill and to recommend it to the Supreme Soviet of the U.S.S.R. for approval. On the basis of the remarks and wishes expressed by the deputies the committee moved a number of amendments to the bill. Since many questions raised in the debates could not be decided without a preliminary study the committee went on record in favour of instructing the Government to take into account the remarks and proposals made by the deputies during the session.

The Supreme Soviet of the U.S.S.R. agreed with these motions and passed a law on changing the system of industrial management and reorganising a number of government bodies with due regard for the committee's amendments.

The Supreme Soviet set up a commission of 97 members for the purpose of elaborating a draft for a new Constitution of the Union of Soviet Socialist Republics. The Constitutional Commission is preparing the draft of the Fundamental Law of the U.S.S.R., which must reflect the new stage in the development of Soviet society and crown the 50 years of history of the Soviet state.

The Presidium of the Supreme Soviet of the U.S.S.R.

The businesslike and comparatively brief functions of the Supreme Soviet require such a government body which in between the sessions of the Supreme Soviet ensures a continuity of state leadership, solves urgent problems, controls the bodies accountable to the Supreme Soviet, etc. This continuously acting higher body of state power is the Presidium of the Supreme Soviet of the U.S.S.R.

The Presidium is elected from among the deputies of the Supreme Soviet of the U.S.S.R. and is completely accountable to it. The Supreme Soviet elects the Presidium at a joint sitting of the Soviet of the Union and the Soviet of Nationalities. The Presidium consists of 37 deputies, namely, the President, 15 Vice-Presidents, one Secretary and 20 members.

Elected to the post of President of the Presidium of the Supreme Soviet were: M. I. Kalinin (January 17, 1938-March 19, 1946); N. M. Shvernik (March 19, 1946-March 15, 1953); K. Y. Voroshilov (March 15, 1953-May 7, 1960) and A. I. Mikoyan (July 15, 1964-December 9, 1965). The President of the Presidium of the Supreme Soviet from May 7, 1960 to July 15, 1964 was L. I. Brezhnev, the present General Secretary of the Central Committee of the Communist Party of the Soviet Union. The President of the Presidium of the Supreme Soviet today (since December 9, 1965) is N. V. Podgorny.

In addition to prominent government and Party leaders people engaged in production, representatives of the Soviet Armed Forces and workers of culture actively participate in the work of the Presidium.

Deputies representing all sections of the country's population are elected to the Presidium of the Supreme Soviet. Thus elected to the Presidium of the Seventh Supreme Soviet of the U.S.S.R. are: V. I. Bolshukhin (chief foreman of the Sredne-Uralsk Copper Works), Z. P. Pukhova (weaver of the Ivanovo Textile Mill), V. M. Kavun and A. I. Kasatkina (collective-farm chairman and chairwoman), A. D. Nutetegryneh (chairwoman of the Chukotsk Area Soviet), M. Jalalov (tractor team leader from Uzbekistan),

S. M. Budyonny (Marshal of the Soviet Union) and Academician I. G. Petrovsky (Rector of Moscow University).

At the same time the Presidium of the Supreme Soviet is a body in which all the Union Republics are directly represented. According to Article 48 of the Constitution, the 15 Vice-Presidents of the Presidium are elected one from each Union Republic. By tradition the Supreme Soviet elects to these posts the Presidents of the Presidiums of the Supreme Soviets of the Union Republics. There are representatives of 18 nationalities in the Presidium of the Seventh Supreme Soviet of the U.S.S.R.

Thus, by its representative character, its social and national composition, the Presidium is, as it were, a small replica of the Supreme Soviet, a collective capable of discharging the complex functions of the supreme organ of state power.

In between the sessions of the Supreme Soviet of the U.S.S.R. the most important problems of political, economic and cultural development, as well as the key issues of international politics, are considered and solved at the sittings of the Presidium.

The meetings of the Presidium are called by its President at least once in two months. The meetings are usually attended by the chairmen of the chambers of the Supreme Soviet; the chairmen of the standing committees, deputies and representatives of state bodies and mass organisations are invited to the sessions. Since the end of the war the number of meetings of the Presidium has considerably increased and the range of questions considered by it has extended.

All members of the Presidium take part in preparing questions for its meetings, the necessary materials and documents being sent to them beforehand.

Questions are submitted to the Presidium of the Supreme Soviet for consideration by the Council of Ministers, the Supreme Court, the Procurator's Office and other state bodies of the U.S.S.R., the higher organs of power of the Union Republics, mass organisations, members of the Presidium and deputies of the Supreme Soviet of the U.S.S.R.

When questions are to be prepared for consideration at its sittings, the Presidium forms working committees headed by a Vice-President, the Secretary or one of the members of the Presidium. These committees concern themselves, for example, with problems of socialist legality, and prepare questions of awards, citizenship and pardon. There have been cases when Presidium committees were organised to elaborate certain bills. For example, the Presidium formed a committee to prepare a bill on ways of recalling deputies of the Supreme Soviet of the U.S.S.R. Since 1938 the Presidium of the Supreme Soviet has set up a total of 18 different committees.

The meetings of the Presidium of the Supreme Soviet are conducted by the President of the Presidium or one of the Vice-Pres-

Chairman of the Soviet of the Union I. Spiridonov plays host to a delegation from the National Congress of the Republic of Chile

idents. Both the President and the Secretary of the Presidium together sign all the legislative acts of the Supreme Soviet of the U.S.S.R. and the decrees and decisions of the Presidium.

The President, Vice-President, Secretary and members of the Presidium receive and interview citizens, and attend to their letters, proposals, applications and complaints.

The Secretary of the Presidium watches the preparation and drawing up of the decrees passed by the Presidium and supervises the work of the staff employed by the chambers of the Supreme Soviet, its Presidium and the standing committees. Representatives of government bodies, mass, scientific and other organisations assist this staff as consultants.

Article 48 of the Constitution emphasises that for all its activities the Presidium is accountable to the Supreme Soviet of the U.S.S.R. This means that the Supreme Soviet may at any time ask for a report on the activities of the Presidium or a report on the work of individual members of the Presidium.

One of the forms of accounting to the country's supreme representative body is reporting on the decrees passed by the Presidium in between sessions of the Supreme Soviet and requiring its approval. Since the adoption of the present Constitution such reports of the Presidium were considered at 34 sessions of the Supreme Soviet of the U.S.S.R.

The Constitution and other laws of the U.S.S.R. invest the Presidium of the Supreme Soviet of the U.S.S.R. with great powers.

In the first place it is necessary to note the powers of the Presidium as a body that is responsible for the election of deputies to the Supreme Soviet of the U.S.S.R.

The basic rules for elections to the Supreme Soviet of the U.S.S.R. are incorporated in the Constitution. The Presidium of the Supreme Soviet works out and approves the Regulations for Election to the Supreme Soviet of the U.S.S.R. on the basis of and in complete conformity with the Constitution.

After the expiry of its term of office or in the event of dissolution of the Supreme Soviet the Presidium of the Supreme Soviet appoints the time for new elections not later than two months after the expiry of its term of office or dissolution. Decrees of the Presidium of the Supreme Soviet set the polling day and form constituencies for election to the Supreme Soviet of the U.S.S.R. The Presidium approves the membership of the Central Election Commission, establishes uniform ballots and determines the order of keeping the election documents.

At its sittings the Presidium discusses the preparations for the election to the Supreme Soviet of the U.S.S.R. and the observance of the Soviet electoral legislation.

On May 23, 1966, the Presidium of the Supreme Soviet heard a report of the Central Election Commission on the preparations for the election to the Supreme Soviet of the U.S.S.R. It instructed the Presidiums of the Supreme Soviets of the Union Republics to help the Executive Committees of the local Soviets, district and primary election commissions in preparing for the election to the Supreme Soviet of the U.S.S.R.

The Presidium also issues decrees on holding elections in individual constituencies in the event of the death or recall of a deputy elected in a particular constituency.

Under the Constitution the newly elected Supreme Soviet is convened by its Presidium not later than three months after the election. The Constitution empowers the Presidium to call the regular sessions of the Supreme Soviet. The Presidium may also call extraordinary sessions at its discretion or by request of one of the Union Republics.

Before calling the sessions the Presidium has to do extensive and multifarious work preparing the questions submitted to the Supreme Soviet of the U.S.S.R. for consideration.

According to established constitutional practice the Presidium of the Supreme Soviet may submit its own questions to be discussed by the Supreme Soviet. It acts as one of the bodies enjoying the power to legislate.

As was already mentioned, considerable preparations for the sessions of the Supreme Soviet are made by the standing committees of the Soviet of the Union and the Soviet of Nationalities. The Presidium of the Supreme Soviet cannot but take part in this work. An important feature of the Presidium is that it co-ordinates the work of both chambers. In between the sessions of the Supreme Soviet the Presidium directs and co-ordinates the activities of the standing committees.

In some cases the Presidium directly instructs the standing committees to elaborate a particular bill. Thus in 1956 the Legislative Proposals Committees were instructed to prepare a draft Statute of the Supreme Court of the U.S.S.R.

In other cases the Presidium refers to the standing committees for consideration of bills or legislative proposals already submitted to the Supreme Soviet. For example, the bill on the Fundamentals of Civil Legislation of the U.S.S.R. and the Union Republics was referred to the Legislative Proposals Committees for consideration.

Sometimes the Presidium refers certain questions for a conclusion to the standing committees. Thus the question of extending the powers of the Union Republics in the sphere of legislation was referred to the Legislative Proposals Committees for a conclusion and then the bill prepared by the committees was sent to the Presidiums of the Supreme Soviets of the Union Republics for their suggestions.

International treaties subject to ratification are usually referred to the Foreign Affairs Committees for their conclusion.

As was noted at the First Session of the Seventh Supreme Soviet of the U.S.S.R., the formation of new committees in the chambers necessitates the work of co-ordination of the activities of all the committees, the purposeful utilisation of their efforts and potentialities, i.e., it requires further development of the guiding and co-ordinating work of the Presidium of the Supreme Soviet.

The efforts made in this direction by the Presidium are clearly attested by the Decision on the Ways of Elaborating Bills in the Legislative Proposals Committees of the Soviet of the Union and the Soviet of Nationalities, passed by the Presidium on December 20, 1966. The Presidium established that the Fundamentals of legislation should be drafted by the Legislative Proposals Committees jointly with the relevant sectoral committees. In checking up on the fulfilment of its instructions the Presidium of the Supreme Soviet hears reports of the corresponding standing committees. In January 1965 it heard the committee's reports on the drafting of the Fundamentals of Matrimonial Law, the Fundamentals of Legislation on Land Use, and the Fundamentals of Corrective Labour Legislation.

The standing committees of the chambers often submit their own proposals to the Presidium of the Supreme Soviet. As was stated above, in December 1964 the Presidium considered the Legislative Proposals Committees' note on the observance of the Law on Universal Compulsory Eight-Year Schooling. The Presidium approved the recommendations and issued a number of instructions to the all-Union and republican government bodies. On the proposal of the Committees a Decree on Free Transportation for Schoolchildren Living in Rural Areas was passed on July 9, 1965.

Sometimes the Presidium of the Supreme Soviet works together with the standing committees of the chambers. For example, in accordance with the instructions of the chambers of the Supreme Soviet, the Presidium is now working with the chairmen of the chambers and the standing committees on a draft of the Statute of the Standing Committees of the Soviet of the Union and the Soviet of Nationalities.

The Presidium also discharges important functions during the sessions of the Supreme Soviet. It co-ordinates the organisational activities of the chambers, prepares the necessary documents and information materials for the deputies, organises consultations, etc.

The Presidium of the Supreme Soviet renders considerable aid to the deputies also in between the sessions of the Supreme Soviet. It sends to the ministries and departments the deputies' proposals, controls the realisation of these proposals, and helps the deputies in the work in their constituencies.

It is the duty of the Presidium to publish the laws and other acts passed by the Supreme Soviet of the U.S.S.R. in the languages of the Union Republics. The Presidium supervises the publishing of the verbatim reports of the sessions and publishes the *Gazette of the Supreme Soviet of the U.S.S.R.* and the newspaper *Izvestia.*

In between the sessions of the Supreme Soviet the Presidium decides many important questions. When necessary, the Presidium introduces changes into the laws in force, these changes having to be subsequently approved by the Supreme Soviet of the U.S.S.R.

In the sphere of state development the Presidium considers and decides questions pertaining to the system and competence of central government bodies, the interrelations between the Union Republics, the generalisation and popularisation of their experience.

The Presidium forms or reorganises ministries and central departments and classifies them as either all-Union or Union-Republican. Thus by Decree of February 21, 1967, it formed four Union-Republican ministries, namely, building of enterprises of the heavy industry, industrial construction, civil construction and agricultural construction, and instructed the Government to prepare a list of enterprises and organisations to be transferred to these ministries.

The Constitution empowers the Presidium to dismiss and appoint ministers of the U.S.S.R. upon representation of the Chairman of the Council of Ministers in between the sessions of the Supreme Soviet, pending subsequent approval by the Soviet Parliament. The Presidium also elects and dismisses members of the Supreme Court of the U.S.S.R.

Chairman of the Soviet of Nationalities Y. Paletskis talks with a delegation from the Swedish Riksdag

The Constitution grants the higher government bodies of the U.S.S.R. the right to approve changes in the borders between the Union Republics and to approve the formation of new Autonomous Republics and Autonomous Regions within the Union Republics. In practice these important questions are decided by the Presidium of the Supreme Soviet of the U.S.S.R. By representation of the Union Republics the Presidium issued some 20 decrees on these questions between 1953 and 1966. Later these decrees were considered and approved by the Supreme Soviet. Thus, for example, to meet the wishes of the working people of the Tuva Autonomous Region, in accordance with the principle of self-determination of the nationalities and to provide conditions for the further state development of the Tuvinian people, the Presidium of the Supreme Soviet of the U.S.S.R. approved the Decree of the Presidium of the Supreme Soviet of the R.S.F.S.R. to transform the Tuva Autonomous Region into the Tuva Autonomous Soviet Socialist Republic. The Decree of the Presidium of the Supreme Soviet of the U.S.S.R. of October 10, 1961, was later approved by the Supreme Soviet of the U.S.S.R.

The unity of the country's system of Soviets requires that some of the main problems of Soviet development, common to all Union Republics, should be solved uniformly.

In this connection the Presidium of the Supreme Soviet of the U.S.S.R. analyses the activities of the Soviets and adjusts their competence. In 1954 the Presidium decided the question of enlarging rural Soviets and of raising salaries of their chairmen and secretaries. A number of questions within the competence of local Soviets were adjusted by the Decree of the Presidium of the Supreme Soviet of the U.S.S.R. of June 21, 1961, on a Further Restriction of the Administrative Imposition of Fines, by the Decision of September 25, 1964, which determined the order of naming or renaming administrative-territorial units, by the Model Statute of Committees Dealing with Juveniles, approved by the Presidium, and by a number of other decisions of the Presidium.

In some cases the Presidium of the Supreme Soviet of the U.S.S.R. itself decided questions of specific activities of local Soviets. For example, it discussed questions concerning the consideration of applications and complaints of citizens by the Executive Committees of Soviets in Krasnodar Territory, the work of government bodies in Alma Ata and Semipalatinsk Regions of the Kazakh Republic pertaining to aiding and providing for the families of fallen soldiers, to violations of socialist law in the decisions of local Soviets, etc.

The decisions of the Presidium of the Supreme Soviet of the U.S.S.R. help to direct the activities of local government bodies. An important role is also played by the recommendations of the Presidium of the Supreme Soviet given on the basis of the common experience of the Union Republics in solving various problems of Soviet development and on the basis of the statistical data on the mass organisational work furnished by local Soviets. It should be noted that at the Sixth Session of the Supreme Soviet (October 1965) some deputies emphasised the necessity of extending the Presidium's activities aimed at generalising the working experience of the Soviets.

In between the sessions of the Supreme Soviet the Presidium decides a large number of questions pertaining to the management of the national economy. These include primarily finances and the budget. The taxation of enterprises and citizens is regulated by decrees of the Presidium. The Presidium fixes the rates of state duty, the rules for compulsory insurance contributions, and tax and duty rebates.

A correct tax policy plays an important part in stimulating socialist production. Suffice it to refer to the Decree of the Presidium of the Supreme Soviet of the U.S.S.R. of April 10, 1965, on the Collective-Farm Income Tax. This decree established a new principle of taxing the incomes of collective farms, namely, that a tax could be imposed only upon the net income of a collective farm. This approach to taxation offers the collective farms wide scope for boosting their production, raising labour productivity and developing their initiative and the initiative of the collective farmers.

The Presidium also decides many other questions of economic construction. Such are the recent decrees of the Presidium of the

Supreme Soviet on the participation of state and collective farms, industrial, transport and other enterprises and organisations in the building and repairing of highways, on the order of transferring pilot enterprises from local or republican jurisdiction to all-Union jurisdiction, on the reorganisation of the long-term investment banks, etc.

Sometimes the decrees of the Presidium of the Supreme Soviet decide a complex of questions pertaining to a whole branch of economy. Such a decree, for example, is the Air Code of the U.S.S.R. approved on December 26, 1961. The Code determines the principles governing civil aviation and aeronautics for the purpose of safeguarding the interests of the state, ensuring flying safety and satisfying the needs of the national economy and citizens.

The Presidium of the Supreme Soviet also deals with concrete questions of the jurisdiction of industrial and agricultural enterprises, construction jobs and organisations. In accordance with Article 76 of the Constitution of the U.S.S.R. the Presidium, by its decrees, transfers various enterprises, by consent of Union Republics, from the jurisdiction of these Republics to the jurisdiction of the U.S.S.R.

The Presidium of the Supreme Soviet of the U.S.S.R. always devoted particular attention to further improving the welfare of the Soviet people.

Its decisions cover a wide range of measures concerned with pensions, working and living conditions, social security, government aid to mothers of large families and unmarried mothers. The Decree of March 26, 1956, increased the maternity leave, and the Decrees of August 15, 1955, May 26, 1956, and December 13, 1956, provided measures for protecting the labour of young people and established a six-hour work day for them. The Decree of March 6, 1965, increased the pensions of war veterans. Many more such examples could be cited.

The Presidium of the Supreme Soviet is doing a good deal of work in strengthening socialist legality, protecting the rights of Soviet citizens and combating crime and infringement of the law.

In recent years it passed several decrees establishing severer punishment for grave crimes. Such, for example, is the Decree on Greater Criminal Responsibility for Bribery aimed at eradicating all forms of bribery.

The Decree of the Presidium on Increasing the Responsibility for Encroachment upon the Life, Health and Dignity of Militiamen and Their Voluntary Helpers was inspired by concern for the personal inviolability of those who watch over the peace of the Soviet people and maintain law and order.

Considering the numerous wishes and demands of working people, mass organisations and government bodies for eradication of hooliganism, the Presidium of the Supreme Soviet issued on July 26, 1966, the Decree on Increasing the Responsibility for Hooliganism.

An important role in combating careless handling of public property and wasteful spending of state resources is played by the decrees of the Presidium of the Supreme Soviet establishing responsibility for a criminally negligent operation and storage of farm machinery, as well as for exaggerating and otherwise misrepresenting the records of plan fulfilment.

The decrees of the Presidium of the Supreme Soviet regulate some aspects of the housing, labour, matrimonial and hereditary relations of Soviet citizens. This is manifest, for example, in the following statutes approved by the Presidium: the Statute of Considering Labour Disputes, the Statute of the Rights of Factory and Office Trade Union Committees, etc.

The Presidium of the Supreme Soviet is carrying on extensive legal codification, i.e., work connected with abrogation of obsolete laws and preparation and approval of new laws regulating the most diverse aspects of socialist social relations.

The Presidium plays an important part in strengthening the country's defence potential and in building its Armed Forces. By its decrees the Presidium determines the legal statutes of servicemen, the system of directing the Armed Forces, the military service, the measures aimed at enhancing military discipline, keeping military records, and strictly observing the oath of allegiance, etc.

By the Decree of August 23, 1960, the Presidium approved the now effective Disciplinary Regulations and Internal Service Regula-

The British Prime Minister Harold Wilson visits President Podgorny
in the Kremlin

tions of the Armed Forces of the U.S.S.R., and by the Decree of August 22, 1963—the Garrison and Guard Duty Regulations of the Armed Forces of the U.S.S.R. The Decree of August 5, 1960, approved the Statute of Guarding the State Borders of the U.S.S.R.

If an extraordinary situation arises in between the sessions of the highest representative body of power, the Constitution empowers the Presidium of the Supreme Soviet to decide the questions of war and peace.

In between the Supreme Soviet sessions the Presidium declares a state of war in case of a military attack on the U.S.S.R. or a necessity of meeting international commitments of mutual defence against aggression. In some areas or over the entire territory the Presidium may declare martial law to defend the country or to maintain public order and state security. The Presidium has the right to declare a total or partial mobilisation. On the very first day of the war against the fascist hordes which perfidiously invaded the territory of the U.S.S.R. without declaring war, the Presidium of the Supreme Soviet issued a Decree on Martial Law, which stipulated a number of emergency measures to be taken during the armed struggle of the Soviet people against the Hitlerite invasion.

The discharge of the foreign policy functions of the Soviet state, the pursuit of its peaceful policies and the increased co-operation with other countries form part of the activities of the Presidium of the Supreme Soviet of the U.S.S.R.

In accordance with the Constitution the Presidium ratifies or denounces international treaties, conventions and agreements concluded by the Soviet Union. During the term of office of the Sixth Supreme Soviet of the U.S.S.R. alone the Presidium issued 85 decrees ratifying international treaties, agreements, conventions, protocols and other important international instruments aimed at strengthening peace and peaceful co-operation, and developing the economic and cultural relations between the Soviet Union and other countries.

The Presidium of the Supreme Soviet determines the order of observing the international agreements signed by the U.S.S.R. Suffice it to refer to the Decree of September 12, 1958, on the Implementation of the Court Rulings of the Countries with which the U.S.S.R. Has Agreements of Rendering Legal Aid.

Expressing the will of the Soviet people the Presidium responds to the most important international events by voicing its authoritative opinion.

When the forces of international reaction tried to whitewash the Hitlerite war criminals under the plea of Statute-barred crimes, the voice of the Presidium of the Supreme Soviet resounded indignantly. The Presidium emphasised that the Soviet people who suffered the greatest losses in the war could not allow the nazi barbarians to go unpunished. In accordance with the universally recognised standards of international law the Presidium ruled in its Decree of March 14,

This photograph was taken on November 4, 1966, after the French Ambassador to the U.S.S.R. M. Wormser had presented his credentials to President Podgorny

1965 that the nazi criminals guilty of the most outrageous crimes against peace and humanity are indictable and subject to punishment regardless of the time that elapsed since the perpetration of the crimes.

The Appeal of the Presidium of the Supreme Soviet of the U.S.S.R., the Central Committee of the Communist Party of the Soviet Union and the Soviet Government to the governments, parliaments and peoples of all countries on the occasion of the 20th anniversary of the victory over fascist Germany, issued in May 1965, has found a broad response throughout the world.

The Presidium of the Supreme Soviet promotes inter-parliamentary relations, forms the Supreme Soviet delegations to foreign countries and receives the foreign parliamentary and other delegations, as well as individual foreign statesmen and public figures.

The Presidium regularly hears the reports of the delegations returned from abroad and passes decisions on them. The proposals contained in the reports of the delegations are often referred to the appropriate ministries and departments for consideration.

On December 20, 1966, the Presidium of the Supreme Soviet discussed the reports on the journeys to Great Britain and Cambodia made by the Supreme Soviet delegations headed by deputies G. I. Voronov and P. N. Demichev. At the same sitting N. V. Podgorny made a detailed report on his state visit to the Austrian Republic.

Delegations of the Soviet Parliamentary Group make regular reports to the Presidium of the Supreme Soviet on the work of Plenary Conferences and other bodies of the Inter-Parliamentary Union.

As regards solving problems of political, economic and cultural development and international relations, the Presidium continues the work of the Soviet Parliament.

As the supreme legislative body of the country the Supreme Soviet of the U.S.S.R. is given for consideration and approval all of the Presidium's decrees which make changes in the laws in force, as well as the decrees whose approval is directly provided for by the Constitution.

Continuing the activities of the Supreme Soviet in between the sessions and acting as one of the higher independent bodies of state power the Presidium exercises supreme control over the observance of the Constitution and the laws of the U.S.S.R., as well as the activities of the higher administrative, judicial and procurator's bodies.

The Presidium makes sure that the Constitutions and laws of the Union Republics correspond to the Constitution and laws of the U.S.S.R. In the very few cases when a law of a Union Republic failed to correspond to the all-Union law the Presidium of the Supreme Soviet of the U.S.S.R. instructed the Presidium of the Supreme Soviet of the particular Republic to eliminate this discrepancy.

By exercising control over the correspondence between the laws of the Union Republics and the all-Union laws the Presidium of the Supreme Soviet of the U.S.S.R. checks up on the way the Union Republics carry out the instructions of a legislative character contained in the instruments of the Supreme Soviet of the U.S.S.R. or its Presidium. For example, in connection with the passage of the all-Union laws of December 8, 1961, on approving the Fundamentals of Civil Legislation of the U.S.S.R. and the Union Republics and on approving the Fundamentals of Civil Procedure of the U.S.S.R. and the Union Republics, the Supreme Soviets of the Union Republics were instructed to bring the laws of the Union Republics into accord with the Fundamentals. The Presidium of the Supreme Soviet of the U.S.S.R. twice heard reports on the fulfilment of these instructions and issued corresponding decisions in which it was noted that the adoption of civil and civil procedure codes and other acts was the result of the codification of the republican civil legislation and civil procedure legislation laws in accordance with all-Union laws.

In some cases the Presidium of the Supreme Soviet of the U.S.S.R. instructs the Presidiums of the Supreme Soviets of Union Republics to submit proposals on the application of all-Union and republican laws.

In accordance with Article 49 of the Constitution of the U.S.S.R. the Presidium interprets the laws in force. By way of explanation and interpretation it has issued about 25 decrees and decisions. The Presidium gives these explanations on application of laws in response to the requests of citizens, government bodies and mass organisations.

In September 1965 the Presidium of the Supreme Soviet of the U.S.S.R. explained with regard to Article 10 of the Statute of the Rights of Factory and Office Trade Union Committees, that the management cannot dismiss factory, office and professional workers without the consent of their local trade·union committee, except in a small number of cases expressly specified in the Decision of the Presidium of the Supreme Soviet of the U.S.S.R.

An essential prerogative of the Presidium of the Supreme Soviet is also its right to conduct a referendum on its own initiative or by request of one of the Union Republics. It may refer to the people questions requiring a nation-wide discussion and approval, as well as the most important bills.

In accordance with the law the Presidium of the Supreme Soviet controls the work of the following bodies accountable to it: the Council of Ministers, the Supreme Court and the Procurator-General of the U.S.S.R.

The Presidium hears reports and communications of the Supreme Court, the Procurator-General, various ministries or the Government as a whole. The Supreme Court and the Procurator-General of the U.S.S.R. regularly report to the Presidium on strengthening socialist law and combating crime.

The right of the Presidium to rescind the Government's decisions, if they are at variance with the law, is closely connected with the control of the activities of the bodies accountable to the Presidium. The Presidium may also revoke the orders and instructions of the Procurator-General of the U.S.S.R.

The Constitution of the U.S.S.R. grants the following powers to the Presidium as the collective head of the Soviet state: establishment of military, diplomatic and other special ranks; appointment and replacement of the high command of the Armed Forces; appointment and recall of Soviet plenipotentiaries abroad. The Presidium of the Supreme Soviet of the U.S.S.R. institutes orders and medals of the U.S.S.R., establishes honorary titles of the U.S.S.R. and awards prizes and honorary titles.

Representing the Soviet Union in international relations, the Presidium of the Supreme Soviet receives the credentials and letters of recall of accredited foreign diplomatic representatives. The heads of foreign embassies and missions present their credentials to the President or Vice-President of the Presidium in the Kremlin. The foreign ambassadors are accompanied on these occasions by high officials of the diplomatic and in some cases trade missions. The credentials are usually presented in the presence of the Secretary of the Presidium, a representative of the U.S.S.R. Ministry of Foreign Affairs and other government officials.

In accordance with the established tradition the person presenting his credentials and the one receiving them exchange speeches. In these speeches they touch upon the main aspects of the relations between the U.S.S.R. and the state whose representative is presenting his credentials. After the presentation of the credentials the Soviet leaders and the ambassador (envoy) usually engage in a conversation in which they touch upon questions that are of interest to both countries.

When accrediting foreign diplomatic representatives, the Presidium of the Supreme Soviet of the U.S.S.R. makes provisions for their activities and grants them privileges and immunities for discharging their functions in accordance with the rules of international law. These questions are regulated, in particular, in the Statute of Foreign Diplomatic and Consular Representatives on the Territory of the U.S.S.R., approved by a Decree of the Presidium of May 23, 1966.

The Presidium systematically considers proposals for appointing and releasing plenipotentiary representatives of the U.S.S.R. in foreign countries.

The Constitution of the U.S.S.R. empowers the Presidium of the Supreme Soviet, in addition to its other prerogatives, to grant par-

His Majesty Emperor of Ethiopia Haile Sellasie and President Podgorny in the Kremlin, February 27, 1967

dons. It also has the right to issue amnesty decrees. The consideration of these questions by the Presidium pursues the aim of re-educating and correcting persons guilty of offences.

Since its existence the Presidium has issued decrees of amnesty on the occasion of the 20th Anniversary of the Workers' and Peasants' Red Army (January 24, 1938), of the victory over Hitler Germany (July 7, 1945), of the 40th Anniversary of the Great October Socialist Revolution (November 1, 1957) and a number of other analogous acts.

In addition to issuing amnesty decrees, which apply to groups of citizens, the Presidium pardons individual convicts who have firmly embarked on the path of correction and have demonstrated it by their conscientious attitude to work and exemplary behaviour. The Presidium grants pardons to persons convicted by Judicial Collegiums of the Supreme Court of the U.S.S.R., court-martials and courts of law of two or more Union Republics.

The Presidium decides questions of Soviet citizenship. In accordance with the all-Union Law of August 19, 1938, it considers applications for Soviet citizenship from persons living abroad, applications of renouncement of Soviet citizenship, as well as representations for depriving certain persons of Soviet citizenship.

Hundreds of letters from working people are received every day by the Presiduim of the Supreme Soviet and its President. The letters contain applications, complaints and personal requests. At the same time the number of letters containing proposals on boosting the national economy, improving the state apparatus and strengthening socialist legality is increasing with each passing year. The citizens often report on shortcomings in the work of local government bodies and raise questions of eliminating bureaucratic perversions and red tape.

The Presidium gives careful consideration to all letters. Some of the questions are decided at once, while for the settlement of others the letters are referred to ministries, departments, republican and other government bodies. To check up on the facts cited in the letters and applications, officials from the staff of the Presidium of the Supreme Soviet go to different localities.

Many people apply to the Presidium of the Supreme Soviet personally on questions of importance to them. In the Moscow Reception Room of the Presidium each visitor is given a chance to state his case in detail. The visitors are interviewed by members of the staff and are given necessary consultations, explanations and advice. The visitors are received by one of the Vice-Presidents of the Presidium, who take turns working in Moscow, and other members of the Presidium.

Many of the letters received from people, their proposals and wishes are referred to the standing committees of the chambers of the Supreme Soviet and the departments of the Presidium, where the

President Podgorny awards the Gold Star of Hero of Socialist Labour and the Order of Lenin to Academician Nikolai Semyonov

opinions of the citizens are taken into account in the preparation of bills, conclusions on the budget and plan, and in the check-up on the work of ministries and other government bodies.

To discharge all these complex and multifarious functions the Presidium of the Supreme Soviet of the U.S.S.R. has a staff consisting of specialists engaged in various branches of the national economy and culture, government workers and lawyers.

This staff provides the organisational and technical services and prepares the necessary data, reference and other materials on questions considered by the Supreme Soviet of the U.S.S.R., its Presidium and standing committees.

The Presidium of the Supreme Soviet comprises the Secretariat, Reception Office and departments on the work of the Soviets, legal, awards, international relations, and catering for the standing committees. There are special groups of workers engaged in rendering services to the standing committees of the chambers, preparing materials on questions of pardon, citizenship, protocol work, publishing and translating laws, furnishing information on legislation, and rendering financial and economic services.

The work of the staff is supervised by the Secretary of the Presidium of the Supreme Soviet.

Deputies and Electors

Close links between deputies and electors set socialist democracy apart from any other. Article 142 of the Constitution of the U.S.S.R. says that every deputy must report to his electors on his own work and the work of the Soviet to which he has been elected, and that he can be recalled at any time upon decision of a majority of the electors. The rights and duties of a deputy to the Supreme Soviet of the U.S.S.R. and his work in his constituency, in all its diversity of form and method, stem from this basic principle of accountability to the electorate and responsibility towards them.

The deputy is expected to settle and solve the most diverse problems in the lives of the working people belonging to his constituency. He studies their needs and wishes, and receives mandates from them. The deputies, expounding to their electors the laws and other decisions passed by the Supreme Soviet of the U.S.S.R., organise them for the implementation of these enactments; they study the application of these laws in practice and sum up the electors' proposals, aimed at improving Soviet legislation and the work of the state apparatus, for the Supreme Soviet's consideration.

Deputies keep their electors fully informed of the work of the Supreme Soviet and of the results of its sessions.

"In my work as a deputy," says V. P. Grishin, director of Proshursky state farm in Udmurt A.S.S.R., "I try to use any opportunity I have to inform my electors of the Supreme Soviet's decisions and to mobilise them for their implementation. My official reports to the constituency apart, I pursue this line at the sittings of the District and Village Soviets, at the different meetings and conferences, and at my meetings with electors in collective and state farms, and in factory shops."

The personal experiences of deputies as participants in the work of the Supreme Soviet invariably evoke the liveliest interest among the listeners. And so the deputies do their best to satisfy the electorate's curiosity. In Turkmenia, for instance, meetings with the deputies were arranged in all the constituencies following the Second Session of the Seventh Supreme Soviet of the U.S.S.R. At these meetings, the deputies told their listeners all about the session at which the Supreme Soviet had approved the plan of economic development and the State Budget of the U.S.S.R. for 1967. Among the deputies who took part in these meetings were B. Ovezov and V. Rykov—secretaries of the Central Committee of the Communist Party of Turkmenia, A. Klychov—President of the Supreme Soviet Presidium of the Turkmen S.S.R., G. Kisunko—Corresponding Member of the Academy of Sciences of the U.S.S.R., N. Vaskova—team leader at the Ashkhabad construction trust and B. Khojageldiyeva—carpet weaver employed at a Turkmen carpet factory.

As a rule, constituencies are very large, with a population numbering hundreds of thousands, and even millions in some of the constituencies voting for the Soviet of Nationalities. In order to keep as many electors as possible informed of the work of the Supreme Soviet of the U.S.S.R. district and city meetings are held. Industrial enterprises, offices, collective and state farms delegate their representatives to these meetings who, on return, share their information with their colleagues. The Orekhovo-Zuyevo constituency for the elections to the Soviet of the Union includes the towns of Orekhovo-Zuyevo, Pavlovsky Posad and two whole districts. A general meeting of electors was held in Orekhovo-Zuyevo on December 28, 1966, at which a report on the work of the Second Session of the Seventh Supreme Soviet was made by deputy V. V. Grishin. The meeting approved the session's decisions and promised to spare no effort for the successful fulfilment of the second year's targets of the five-year plan.

Needless to say, the deputies of the Supreme Soviet of the U.S.S.R. extend their contacts with the electors well beyond these general meetings. The majority are employed at factories, collective and state farms, enterprises, institutions or organisations situated in their constituency and so they are in daily contact with their electors. And in this lies the efficiency of Soviet deputies. The Kharkov city constituency No. 58 for the elections to the Soviet of Nationalities nominated Hero of Socialist Labour N. Miroshnichenko, lathe operator at the Kharkov Tractor Works. It is a huge constituency, there is plenty of work for a deputy of a city as big as Kharkov, but Miroshnichenko copes with his duties excellently. On return from a session of the Supreme Soviet he always speaks before his electors, telling them what problems had been discussed and what they must do to carry the adopted decisions through. He also speaks on the local radio and on television. Two Thursdays a month Miroshnichenko devotes wholly to his electors, receiving them in the offices of the District Soviet. These are his official reception days, but his electors come to see him at any other time as well, bringing their proposals, requests and complaints to him, or seeking his advice and help. In a month Miroshnichenko receives hundreds of letters, and answers every one of them. The life experience he has gained as a working man and his daily contacts with people enable him to pose questions of cardinal importance before the state bodies, such as: ways and means of removing shortcomings in building of co-operative dwellings; speeding up the cultural development of the villages; providing the youth with more cultural facilities for their leisure hours; improving the railway service for out-of-town workers, and so on.

Some deputies of the Supreme Soviet of the U.S.S.R. have one official reception day a week, others have one every fortnight. The day and the hours when the residents can come to see their deputy are announced in the local newspaper or over the local radio, and notices are also posted in the local Soviets. In Kalinin, for instance, there is a notice on the building of the City Executive Committee which says: "Deputy of the Supreme Soviet of the U.S.S.R. Alexandra Alexandrovna Yevseyeva will receive electors every 16th and 30th of the month from midday on." Alexandra Yevseyeva is a team leader at the Kalinin factory of artificial leather. On some days she receives as many as twenty electors.

Deputy V. I. Zaitseva, who heads a chair at the Tajik State Medical Institute, and is a merited doctor and scientist of the Tajik Republic, receives her electors every Wednesday, in addition to which she goes out to the Gissar, Kuibyshev, Lenin and Regar districts twice a month to receive her electors resident there. The population is notified of her reception days through the radio and the local newspapers. In the interval between the First and Second sessions of the Seventh Supreme Soviet, V. Zaitseva held eight reception days in these districts and addressed five meetings of electors.

Colonel-General G. B. Baklanov, another deputy of the Supreme Soviet of the U.S.S.R., informed the Presidium that in the course of two years he had received 923 people and investigated 2,803 written complaints and requests, satisfying more than 80 per cent of the latter.

Deputy N. N. Rusakov, a fitter at the Elektrosila factory in Leningrad, receives scores of electors and the postman brings him about a hundred letters a month, none of which are left unanswered.

The electors' letters do not contain personal requests only, they also raise questions which are of concern to the whole community: the need to raise the efficiency of trading organisations, public health institutions, libraries, clubs, schools, enterprises and collective farms, the demand for more hospitals and shops, and so forth.

Here is a typical example. Of the 118 requests received by Y. S. Grosul, President of the Moldavian Academy of Sciences, in the first six months after his election to the Supreme Soviet of the U.S.S.R., 15 called for greater efficiency in the work of collective farms and demanded the purchase of new farming machines for them; 9 mentioned factories that needed help to start smooth production going; 27 wanted help in the work of schools, hospitals, municipal services, trade and catering establishments; 18 dealt with labour protection and citizens' rights; 27 were on housing problems; 22 asked for assistance in procuring building materials for individual house construction in rural districts.

Deputies strive for the fulfilment of their electors' mandates with commendable energy and insistence. The Presidium of the Supreme Soviet of the U.S.S.R. has received the minutes of a meeting held on December 12, 1965, at the Zhdanov collective farm, Aravan District, Osh Region, Kirghiz S.S.R. The meeting was attended by 1,132 electors. They heard and discussed the report of their deputy, Hero of Socialist Labour M. Umarova, a field team leader at the collective farm, on the fulfilment of their mandates. The meeting unanimously praised M. Umarova for her efforts, initiative and perseverance in their behalf. She had indeed achieved a great deal with the support of the local Soviet and Party bodies, collective-farm boards, building and supplies organisations, notably the building of new highways and the repair of the old; the opening of a new bus line between villages; the building of new schools, kindergartens and crèches for a number of collective farms, and a boarding school and a club in a district centre; putting on running water at some of the collective farms and digging artesian wells in the grazing pastures.

Also exemplary in this respect is the work of deputy K. V. Kopysova, director of a hospital in Krasnogorsk District, Udmurt A.S.S.R. She maintains close and constant ties with her electors, and knows their needs and requirements well. Her electors in the different parts of her constituency see her often, and whatever can be done on the spot with their support she always does.

In the Valamaz township, for instance, kindergartens and crèches were a problem. The electors had raised the question frequently. Finally, the local organisations agreed to join forces and try to settle the matter by local means. And they did. The lumber camp administration had an unfinished house: they completed it and opened a kindergarten and crèche for fifty children. The local factory also provided premises for a crèche accommodating fifty babies.

Deputy Kopysova informed the Supreme Soviet of the U.S.S.R. of some of the mandates she had received from her electors. At the Third Session of the Sixth Supreme Soviet, when the subject under discussion was the State Budget of the Soviet Union for 1964, she spoke of the need to increase the allocation of funds to the Udmurt Republic for building and repairing hospitals and schools, and providing the rural hospitals with the necessary apparatus and vehicles. Her request was granted, and the Udmurt Republic was allocated an additional 756,000 rubles for the needs of its health services and public education.

Deputies to the Supreme Soviet of the U.S.S.R. have the right to approach state institutions, enterprises and organisations for information which they may need, preparatory to a session of the Supreme Soviet or a meeting of one of its committees, and which will help them to fulfil their electors' mandates and discharge some of their other duties. The state organs, institutions and mass organisations on their part never deny the deputies their assistance.

Not infrequently, deputies appeal to the Presidium of the Supreme Soviet for help in connection with their electors' mandates, and the necessary measures are taken in each instance.

One of the basic principles of socialist democracy is the responsibility of the deputies before their electors. The Constitution of the U.S.S.R. stipulates that a deputy of the Supreme Soviet must report to his electors on his own work and the work of the Soviet Parliament. Most of the deputies perform this duty regularly. When addressing a meeting of the electorate after the closing of a session they speak of the adopted decisions and also, as a rule, give an account of their own work in the parliament, reporting what they themselves had done for their constituency and how far they had fulfilled their electors' mandates. Here are a few examples.

A regular meeting of voters in the Gagra constituency for the elections to the Soviet of Nationalities, held on March 19, 1965, had the following item on the agenda: "Report by deputy Y. T. Kvitsiniya on his own work and the work of the Supreme Soviet over a period of fifteen months, from January 18, 1964, to March 15, 1965." On June 22-26, 1965, similar meetings were held in the Polog, Vasilyevka, Mikhailovka and Orekhovka districts of Zaporozhye Region. Deputy F. D. Ovcharenko, who heads one of the departments of the Institute of General and Inorganic Chemistry of the Ukrainian Academy of Sciences, reported to his electors on what he had accomplished in the first half-year of 1965. A meeting of the electors in the village Ananyevo and the township Kok-Dubeh, Kirghizia, held on November 14, 1964, was attended by 343 people. They heard and discussed the report of their deputy B. Ryspayev.

The Rovno constituency's deputy to the Soviet of Nationalities is A. F. Fyodorov, twice Hero of the Soviet Union, commander of a guerilla formation in the Ukraine during the war, and now Ukraine's Minister of Social Security. He accounts to his electors regularly. In April 1965 he reported to four meetings, or over two thousand electors, and in January 1966 to three meetings, or roughly fifteen hundred electors. On June 12, 1966, A. F. Fyodorov was elected to the Supreme Soviet of the U.S.S.R. for the seventh time.

Deputies combine their duties with regular work at enterprises, collective and state farms, state institutions or mass organisations, as the case may be. The state pays them a hundred rubles a month to cover their expenses as deputies: travel within the precincts of their constituency, correspondence with electors, with state and mass organisations, arrangements for meetings with their electors, etc. Deputies are permitted to absent themselves from work, without losing their salary or their average earnings, in order to attend sessions of the Supreme Soviet, to work on one of the standing committees, to carry out the assignments given them by the Supreme Soviet of the U.S.S.R., its Presidium, or the relevant standing committee, and also to meet their electors and report to them on their work. Deputies of the Supreme Soviet of the U.S.S.R. wear a special badge and carry a deputy's card. They are entitled to free passage by rail, ship and plane.

The Constitution of the U.S.S.R. guarantees their legal immunity: a deputy of the Supreme Soviet may not be prosecuted or arrested without the consent of the Supreme Soviet of the U.S.S.R. and when the Supreme Soviet is not in session, without the consent of its Presidium.

A deputy is not only accountable but also responsible towards his electors. He may be recalled at any time by decision of the majority in the statutory manner.

The right to recall deputies is widely exercised by electors. Ten deputies were recalled from the Fifth and Sixth Supreme Soviets for either failing to justify the electors' trust in them or for committing actions unworthy of their high calling.

The procedure of recalling a Supreme Soviet deputy is laid down in the law passed on October 30, 1959.

The right to revoke the mandate of a deputy is secured to mass organisations and societies of the working people acting through their central, republican, territory, regional, district or city organs of power, and also to the general meetings of factory or institution staffs, of collective-farm members, and of servicemen. In other words, to the same mass organisations and general meetings of the working people which have the right to nominate a candidate. These collectives, therefore, do not drop matters once they had nominated their candidate, but constantly follow his career to see how well he discharges his duties and to what extent he justifies the confidence placed in him.

The law guarantees the deputy the right to present to the pertinent organ of power or the given collective an explanation of the circumstances, which had led his electors to raise the question of his recall.

The decisions of the mass organisations or the general meetings of the working people to recall their deputy are directed to the Presidium of the Supreme Soviet of the U.S.S.R., which studies the materials presented to it from the legal angle (whether the given general meetings or mass organisations are competent to raise the question of recall, whether the deputy's right to acquit himself has been exercised, and so on). If the Presidium is satisfied, it issues a writ for a vote to be taken for the recall of the deputy in question, publishing its decree in the local press.

Thereupon, a local commission is formed from among the representatives of the mass organisations, the societies of working people and the general meetings, to handle the voting for the recall of their deputy. This commission is made responsible for the observance of the law, for determining the returns and for examining any comptaints that might come in.

The question of recalling a deputy is decided by electors' meetings in the given constituency, held at their place of work (enterprises, offices, collective farms, etc.), in military units or in their place of residence. As a rule, several days are assigned to these meetings.

The law guarantees every mass organisation and every citizen of the U.S.S.R. the right to freely campaign for or against the recall of a deputy. At their meetings, the electors thoroughly discuss the ques-

THE SYSTEM OF SOVIETS OF WORKING PEOPLE'S DEPUTIES

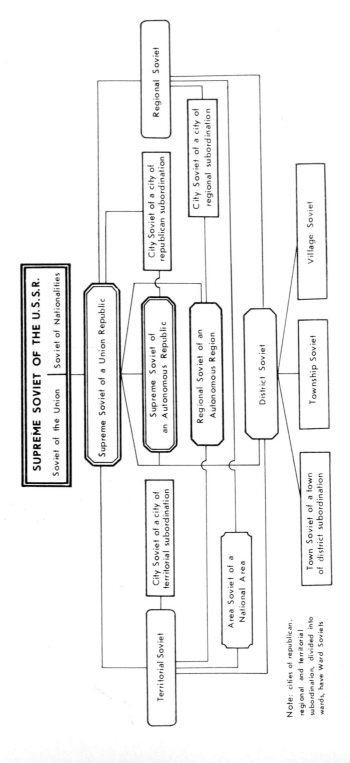

SUPREME SOVIET OF THE U.S.S.R.

Soviet of the Union | Soviet of Nationalities

Supreme Soviet of a Union Republic

Supreme Soviet of an Autonomous Republic

City Soviet of a city of republican subordination

Regional Soviet

City Soviet of a city of regional subordination

Regional Soviet of an Autonomous Region

District Soviet

Village Soviet

Township Soviet

Town Soviet of a town of district subordination

Territorial Soviet

City Soviet of a city of territorial subordination

Area Soviet of a National Area

Note: cities of republican, regional and territorial subordination, divided into wards, have Ward Soviets

tion from every angle, and carefully weigh up all the arguments for and against the deputy's recall.

The results of the open ballot are entered in the minutes of the given meeting which must be presented within three days to the District Election Commission. The votes are then counted with the reference to the minutes of all the meetings held in the constituency, and the commission sums up the results. A deputy is recalled if more than half of the electors living in that constituency have voted for it. The District Commission now presents the results of the voting to the Presidium of the Supreme Soviet of the U.S.S.R. The results must be published by the District Commission not later than five days after they had been determined.

If the deputy is recalled, the Presidium of the Supreme Soviet of the U.S.S.R. will appoint re-elections in that particular constituency within the next two months.

A deputy may go out of office before his term is up not only because he has been recalled. He can also hand in his resignation. It is accepted or declined by the chamber concerned, and in the interval between sessions by the Presidium of the Supreme Soviet of the U.S.S.R.

At the opening of each session of the Soviet of the Union and the Soviet of Nationalities, the Credentials Committees report that such and such deputies have been recalled, have resigned or died, and that other candidates have been elected in their place. The two chambers then examine and approve the credentials of the newly elected deputies.

THE STATE ECONOMIC PLAN
AND THE STATE BUDGET OF THE U.S.S.R.

Under the Constitution the economic life of the Soviet Union is determined and guided by the state economic plan for the purpose of increasing the wealth of society, steadily raising the material and cultural standards of the people, strengthening the independence of the U.S.S.R. and its defence potential. As stated earlier, under the Constitution it is the function of the higher organs of state power and state administration to determine the state economic plan, to endorse the State Budget and to report on its implementation.

The Supreme Soviet of the U.S.S.R. devotes much time and care to the preparation, discussion and settlement of these important questions which affect every aspect of the country's life. In effect, the peoples of the U.S.S.R. empower the Supreme Soviet to manage on their behalf the entire material and spiritual riches of the country.

The State Plan of Economic Development

As the highest organ of state power, the Supreme Soviet of the U.S.S.R. approves, upon examination, the annual plan of the Soviet Union's economic development. The plans are aimed at a further and greater development of socialist production and economic potential, and on this basis at a steady rise of the people's prosperity and cultural level.

The fulfilment of the seven-year plan (1959-1965) and the results of the first eighteen months of the current five-year plan (1966-1970) show that the Soviet people are successfully coping with the tasks set before them by the Communist Party.

In the last eight years a sizable contribution was made to the creation of a material and technical basis of communism, and the economic potential of the country was increased substantially. New natural resources were explored and added to the general economic potential. The fixed productive assets showed an increase of 90 per cent from 1959 to 1965, and the national income of more than 50 per cent.

Industry made a large step forward with the planned enlargement and commissioning of new production capacities.

In 1965 the overall industrial output was worth 234,300 million rubles, or almost double that in 1958.

The pattern of industry was improved, and the branches responsible for the technical re-equipment of Soviet economy as a whole were developed faster than the others. During the seven-year-plan period the production of electric power more than doubled (507,000 million kwh in 1965 as against 235,000 million kwh in 1958). Considerably more electric power was made available to industrial enterprises, construction projects and transport, and more electricity was used by farms and in the home. The Soviet Union is building the largest hydroelectric power stations in the world. The Bratsk hydroelectric power station, on the Angara in Siberia, is the world's biggest, but before long it will cede the palm to the Krasnoyarsk station on the Yenisei which will have a capacity of 6 million kw.

Provision was made in the economic plans of the last years for a rapid development of the chemical industry in the directions outlined by the May 1958 Plenary Meeting of the Central Committee and by other Party decisions. More than 9,000 million rubles were invested in this branch of industry during the seven-year-plan period (1959-1965), or 2.3 times the amount invested in all the foregoing years of Soviet power. In the course of the seven years over five hundred large chemical plants were built and put into operation. Production was more than doubled, and the average annual increment reached 14 per cent, which was 50 per cent higher than the rate of growth of Soviet industry as a whole.

In 1965 the chemical plants produced 801,500 tons of synthetic resin and plastics, as against 10,900 tons in 1940. For output of synthetic fibres the figures were 407,300 tons and 11,100 tons respectively. Production of synthetic rubber, automobile tyres and other rubber goods has been considerably enlarged. The capacities of factories making mineral fertilisers, chemical insecticides and weed killers are growing at a fast pace. For instance, 31,300,000 tons of mineral fertiliser were produced in 1965, as against 3,200,000 in 1940.

Production of metal and fuel, the basis of modern industry, is developing rapidly. The 1965 output of pig iron was 66,200,000 tons, and steel 91 million tons, while in 1958 it was 39.6 million tons and 54.9 million tons respectively.

The extraction of oil and gas is proceeding at an increasingly fast pace, the figures for 1965 being 242.9 million tons of the former and 129,400 million cu m of the latter. Gas mains in the Soviet Union have a total length of over 40,000 kilometres. A number of large oil and gas deposits have recently been discovered in Western Siberia, Western Kazakhstan and Byelorussia.

Work has been launched on the technical reconstruction of all types of transport whose freight turnover in 1965 reached 2,764,000 million tons-km, or a 72 per cent increase over that of 1958. By the end of 1965 more than 80,000 kilometres of railways were switched to electric or diesel traction. The tonnage of the merchant marine has increased substantially. The large fleet of modern aircraft transports thousands of passengers every day.

The light and the food industries showed a 50 per cent increase in production during the seven-year period: fabrics by 1,588 million metres, leather footwear by 130 million pairs, refrigerators by 1,300,000 items and television sets by 2,676,000. A 50 per cent increase was achieved in the production of meat, butter and whole milk products, and that of sugar was doubled.

The national economic plans made provision for a further development of agriculture by building up its material and technical basis and intensification of production. Thus, towards the end of 1965 the farms had 3,032,000 tractors in terms of 15 h.p. units (a 70 per cent increase over the number in 1958), 520,000 combine harvesters, and 982,000 trucks. During that year the farms were supplied with over 27 million tons of mineral fertiliser, and considerably greater quantities of chemical insecticides and weed killers than in previous years.

Capital construction has assumed enormous proportions. In the period 1959-1965 state and co-operative enterprises invested 240,800 million rubles in industry, transport, agriculture, housing, cultural and public services' development, which exceeded the total investments made for the same purpose in all the foregoing years of Soviet power. In the seven-year period roughly 5,500 large new industrial enterprises were put into operation.

The building of new and the enlargement and reconstruction of existing enterprises resulted in the following increase in production capacities: electric power stations by 61 million kwh, coal mining by 120 million tons a year, pig iron by 18.8 million tons a year, steel smelting by 23 million tons a year, leather footwear by 95 million pairs a year, sugar refined from beetroot by 232,600 tons a day. Also, 7,700 kilometres of new railways were built, and 15,200 kilometres of existing railways were electrified.

Priority development of the manufacture of the producer goods promoted the growth of labour productivity. In 1965, as against 1958, per hour productivity in industry was higher by 58 per cent, in building by 72 per cent, and in rail transport by 66 per cent. Thanks to the growth of labour productivity industry as a whole gave a 67 per cent increase in output from 1959 to 1965.

The broad five-year programme of economic and cultural development, outlined in the Directives of the Twenty-Third Party Congress, took off to a good start in 1966. The annual economic plan was overfulfilled in all basic indices: in aggregate volume and rates of growth of industrial production, in output of essential goods, in growth of labour productivity in industry, and in development of transport. Overall agricultural output was 10 per cent higher than the year before, and the grain harvest was equal to 170.8 million tons, which exceeded the annual average yield earmarked for the current five-year period.

The development of economy in accordance with the plans adopted by the Supreme Soviet of the U.S.S.R. provides the basis for the steady improvement of the Soviet people's well-being and cultural standards.

In the seven years from 1959 to 1965, the real incomes of the population increased by 30 per cent. In 1966, the first year of the current five-year-plan period, the increase was more than 6 per cent per capita. This was achieved by raising the wages of industrial and office workers and the pay of collective farmers, and by increasing public consumption funds, which cover the cost of the population's free medical aid, free education, benefits, pensions, student maintenance grants, annual holidays, free or partially free accommodation in health homes, holiday homes, and so forth.

In 1959-1966, the population received over 245,000 million rubles in benefits and grants covered by the public consumption funds. The sum paid out in 1966 was 45,000 million rubles, or almost double that expended in 1958.

In 1966 these funds paid for the education of 72 million people of whom 48 million were school pupils, 4,100,000 were university and institute students, and 4 million attended specialised secondary schools. Over 32 million people receive their pensions from the same source, and 3,500,000 mothers of large families and 1,600,000 unmarried mothers—their monthly allowances. About 8,500,000 children of pre-school age are accommodated in kindergartens and crèches, and over 15,000,000 people a year spend their holidays at holiday homes, boarding houses and summer camps or take a cure at a health home or medical centre. There is a wide network of district polyclinics, out-patient departments, hospitals, maternity and children's consultation clinics, and when needed, doctors are available for home calls at any hour of the day and night. Every single family in the Soviet Union profits in one way or another from the benefits provided by the state at the expense of the public consumption funds.

The Soviet Government is greatly concerned with the need of improving the population's living conditions. Housing development in 1959-1965 has given the urban and rural population 558 million square metres of dwelling space with money provided by the state and the citizens, or as many houses as had been built in all the years of Soviet power up till 1958. During the last ten years practically half of the population moved into new or bigger flats.

As the real incomes increased so did the sale of consumer goods and the population's savings. In 1965 the state and co-operative trading enterprises sold 104,800 million rubles' worth of goods, which was 8,400 million rubles more than in 1964. Retail sales in 1965 included among other things 21,900,000 watches and clocks, 5,000,000 wireless sets and radio gramophones, 3,300,000 TV sets, 1,500,000 refrigerators and 3,100,000 washing machines. And the population deposited three thousand million rubles more in their savings banks than the previous year.

Sitting of the Committee for Industry, Transport and Communications of the Soviet of Nationalities, chaired by Deputy G. Chogovadze on December 14, 1966

At the present time, eight-year school education is compulsory for all, and a decision has been adopted to introduce compulsory ten-year education. No less than 664,000 scientific workers are employed at the research institutes and higher schools in the U.S.S.R.

The Second Session of the Seventh Supreme Soviet of the U.S.S.R. passed a Law on the State Plan of National Economic Development for 1967. The main points of this plan are:

priority development of those branches of industry which will ensure technical progress, and improvement of the pattern of social production;

further development of agriculture by enlarging its material and technical basis, raising crop yield and livestock productivity;

raising the level of technical efficiency in all branches of the national economy, enhancing the role of economic incentives to expand and better production; increasing labour productivity, reducing production costs and increasing profits;

better management of capital construction, concentration of capital investments in priority projects, speeding up the construction and commissioning of production capacities;

raising living and cultural standards, further housing development, improving the system of public education and health protection, satisfying the population's increasing demand for consumer goods and public services.

The Supreme Soviet has set the following targets for 1967:

National income (consumption and accumulation funds)	an increase of	6.6%	compared to 1966
Gross output of industrial production	" "	7.3%	" "
Centralised capital investments	" "	7%	" "
Freight carriage, all means of transport	" "	5.6%	" "
Real incomes per capita	" "	5.5%	" "
Retail sales in state and co-operative trade	" "	7.4%	" "
Building of new dwellings by the state	" "	17%	" "
Number of pupils in schools and in extended-day groups	" "	16.2%	" "
Make-and-mend and other services	" "	17.4%	" "
Accommodation in crèches, kindergartens, etc., maintained by the state	" "	9.9%	" "
Number of students in universities, institutes, etc.	" "	4.3%	" "

Fulfilment of the second year's targets of the five-year plan will ensure a further advance in the country's economic, social and cultural progress.

The State Budget of the U.S.S.R.

The Supreme Soviet of the U.S.S.R. examines and approves the State Budget for the coming year and the report on the execution of the previous year's budget.

Out of this budget funds are allocated for the prompt launching of undertakings approved by the state economic plan and aimed at developing socialist economy and culture, raising the living standards of the population, and strengthening the country's defence potential.

At its Second Session in December 1966, the Seventh Supreme Soviet endorsed the State Budget for 1967 with receipts totalling 110,200 million rubles and expenditures 110,000 million rubles.

In the 1967 budget, 91 per cent of the receipts, or 100,300 million rubles, are compounded of turnover tax, remittances for fixed productive assets and circulating funds, deductions from profits, income and other taxes, payable by state and co-operative enterprises and organisations. Individual income taxes payable by the population make up a mere 8.2 per cent of the budget revenue.

The following expenditures have been approved for 1967:

National economy development	Rbs. 46,900 million
Social and cultural needs	42,900 million
Defence	14,500 million
Maintenance of state administration bodies	1,400 million

Money is allocated for all the undertakings envisaged by the state plan for the development of industry. In 1967 industry will be financed to the extent of 45,700 million rubles, which exceeds the 1966 figure by 7.3 per cent. The budget will allocate 21,900 million rubles and the enterprises and organisations 23,800 million rubles out of their own resources. Large expenditures towards the same end will also be made from bank credits and the enterprises' development funds.

The 1967 allocations for the development of the key branches of heavy industry—electric power production, metallurgy, machine-building, the chemical industry and electronics—amount to 19,300 million rubles, or 42 per cent of the total expenditure on industry.

Allocations for the light, food and local industries and also for the organisation of public services will be increased by 5,200 million rubles, or roughly 19 per cent as against 1966, which will facilitate the fulfilment of the tasks set out in the annual plan for greater output of consumer goods.

Agricultural development is to be allocated 13,500 million rubles this year, of which 6,300 million rubles are to come from the State Budget. The bulk of this money will go towards financing capital investments and thus ensuring a further rapid rise in agricultural production.

The 1967 budget allocations for social and cultural needs equal 42,000 million rubles, or 5.2 per cent more than last year. The main items of expenditure are:

Public education, science and culture	19,600 million rubles
Health protection and physical culture	7,400 " "
Social insurance and social security	15,900 " "

Almost eight thousand million rubles will be used to finance schools and pre-school establishments. Expenditures connected with the development of science will amount to 7,200 million rubles, or 6.3 per cent more than in 1966, allocated in part by the budget and in part by enterprises and organisations. State pensions, benefits and allowances payable out of the budget will this year equal 11,200 million rubles.

The budgets of the Union Republics approved for 1967 amount to 52,700 million rubles, or 47.9 per cent of the State Budget of the U.S.S.R.

	(million)			(million)
R.S.F.S.R	27,696 rubles	Moldavian S.S.R.	600 rubles
Ukrainian S.S.R.	9,899 "	Latvian S.S.R.	655 "
Byelorussian S.S.R.	2,067 "	Kirghiz S.S.R.	600 "
Uzbek S.S.R.	2,225 "	Tajik S.S.R.	539 "
Kazakh S.S.R.	3,984 "	Armenian S.S.R.	639 "
Georgian S.S.R.	980 "	Turkmen S.S.R.	520 "
Azerbaijan S.S.R.	1,008 "	Estonian S.S.R.	455 "
Lithuanian S.S.R.	932 "		

The 1967 budgets of the Union Republics ensure the further economic and cultural development of each separate Republic in accordance with the state economic plan of the U.S.S.R. In order to ensure the realisation of planned projects of a nation-wide significance, the Union Republics will be allocated funds from the all-Union budget in the following amounts: the Uzbek S.S.R. 254.5 million rubles, the Kazakh S.S.R. 892.8 million rubles, and the Turkmen S.S.R. 83.1 million rubles.

Shorter Working Day and Higher Wages

In the last ten years the Supreme Soviet of the U.S.S.R. passed a number of important decisions with the aim of increasing the people's well-being. The Presidium of the Supreme Soviet of the U.S.S.R. in its Decree of March 8, 1956, made the sixth day of the week (preceding holidays or the weekly day-offs) a six-hour working day for the employees of all enterprises, institutions and organisations. The working week was cut down to 41 hours, and even less than that for some categories of workers.

Simultaneously with the general improvement of working conditions, the question of raising and adjusting the pay of workers in industry, construction, state agricultural enterprises and transport was being solved. And on January 1, 1957, the wages of a number of low-paid categories were increased. As a result of all these measures, more than 50 million industrial and office workers received higher wage rates.

On May 7, 1960, the Supreme Soviet of the U.S.S.R. passed a Law on the Abolition of Income Taxes on Wages as a result of which employees earning not more than 60 rubles a month no longer had to pay income tax and the childless tax leviable on bachelors and parents of small families in this low income bracket was also lifted. An average 40 per cent reduction has also been made on income and childless taxes from other categories of workers.

In July 1964, the Fourth Session of the Sixth Supreme Soviet of the U.S.S.R. passed a law on a salary increase for people employed in public education, the health services, and some other professions catering directly to the needs of the population. The average increase was 21 per cent, but to specify:

Employees in public education received a 25 per cent increase, Employees in the health services received a 23 per cent increase, Employees in trade (also cafés, canteens, etc.) received a 18 per cent increase, Employees in municipal services received a 15 per cent increase.

Workers in public education and public health everywhere in the country began to draw a higher salary on September 1, 1964, and for employees in all four categories of public services, working in the northern regions of the Soviet Union the increase came into effect as of October 1964.

As suggested by the Central Committee of the Communist Party and the Council of Ministers of the U.S.S.R., the Fifth Session of the Sixth Supreme Soviet of the U.S.S.R. made provision in the approved state plan of economic development for 1965 and the 1965 State Budget of the U.S.S.R. for the extension of the new wage scale to other branches of public services as well, and also for a speedier introduction of a higher minimum wage, effective throughout the country, than originally planned. As a result, more than eighteen million factory, office and professional workers received an increase in wages.

The Directives of the Twenty-Third Party Congress on the new five-year plan made provision for a further wage increase in 1966-1967 of not less than 20 per cent on the average, and a 35-40 per cent increase in the cash incomes and incomes in kind of collective farmers. The minimum wage for industrial and office workers will be raised to sixty rubles a month, and the middle bracket will also have an increase in wages, both categories being entitled to larger bonuses.

When carrying the above decisions into effect it is intended to improve the remuneration of people working in difficult and harmful conditions, underground, etc.

On March 14, 1967, the Presidium of the Supreme Soviet of the U.S.S.R. issued a decree on changing to a five-day work week with two days off. The purpose is to give Soviet people easier working conditions, to give them a better opportunity of raising their work qualifications and cultural level, to enable them to plan their leisure time in a more profitable manner, and also to achieve a more efficient organisation of social production.

Improved Working Conditions for Women
and Minors

In that same period a number of laws were passed on the further improvement of working conditions for women and minors.

The Supreme Soviet of the U.S.S.R. has established some additional privileges for women workers. By decree of the Presidium of the Supreme Soviet of the U.S.S.R. issued on March 26, 1956, the 77 day leave for expectant mothers increased to 112 days—56 before and 56 after the birth of the child—with statutory payment of a maternity benefit. In the event of complicated delivery or the birth of twins and more, the post-natal leave is extended to 70 days.

Expectant mothers (from the moment pregnancy has been established) and women who have babies less than a year old have the right to change to a job nearer to their homes preserving the continuity of their work record. It is forbidden to give overtime work to women four months pregnant, and to put nursing mothers on night shift.

To give greater labour protection to minors, the Presidium of the Supreme Soviet of the U.S.S.R., by a Decree of December 13, 1956, forbade the employment of youngsters under sixteen years of age. Fifteen-year-olds can be taken on in exceptional cases only, by special agreement with the factory or office trade union committees.

A four-hour working day has been established by law for 15-year-old apprentices and employees, and a six-hour day for employees aged 16 to 18.

By a decree of the Presidium of the Supreme Soviet of the U.S.S.R. dated August 15, 1955, the annual leave of industrial and office workers under eighteen was increased to one calendar month. As a general rule, leave is granted in summer, but they are free to take it at any other time of the year if they so wish.

Higher Pensions

On July 14, 1956, the Supreme Soviet of the U.S.S.R. passed a Law on State Pensions which has considerably benefited the citizens of retiring age. The law increased the size of the pensions substantially, enlarged the circle of people entitled to a pension, established a younger eligibility age for some categories of working people, and so forth. State pensions are paid on three counts: old age, disability, or the loss of the bread-winner.

In the Soviet Union retiring age is 60 for men with a work record of not less than 25 years, and 55 for women with a work record of not less than 20 years.

People who work underground, in harmful conditions or in hot shops are entitled to retire earlier: men at 50, with a work record of not less than 20 years, and women at 45, with a work record of

Sitting of the Committee for Trade and Public Amenities of the Soviet of the Union chaired by Deputy D. Komarova on December 14, 1966. Deputy B. Konoplyov is speaking

not less than 15 years. Disability pensions are paid irrespective of when the recipients became disabled: during work, before they ever began work, or after they gave up work. If a person is disabled as a result of a work accident or a professional disease, he is granted a pension regardless of his length of service. A person who has not worked the required number of years entitling him to a full pension will be paid a proportionately smaller one.

In the Soviet Union pensions are paid wholly from state and social funds. The State Budget allocations include moneys from the social insurance budget, compounded of payments made by enterprises, institutions and organisations. No deductions whatsoever are made from pensions. Pensions are not taxable. Citizens who have a right to a state pension can apply for it as soon as they reach the required age.

After the Law on State Pensions had been passed, the Central Committee of the Communist Party, the Council of Ministers of the U.S.S.R. and the Presidium of the Supreme Soviet of the U.S.S.R. took additional measures to further increase certain categories of pensions. Thus, in 1959 the size of pensions paid to people disabled through pneumoconiosis, an occupational disease, was enlarged. As from May 1, 1965, higher minimum pensions have been granted to first and second group invalids from among privates, sergeants and warrant officers on active service becoming disabled as a result of a wound, shellshock or injury received when defending the U.S.S.R. or performing some other military duty, or again as a consequence of an illness contracted during the war. As from October 1, 1965, the same rule became applicable to first and second class invalids from among the industrial and office workers, servicemen—privates, sergeants and warrant-officers on active service, and also to families who have lost their bread-winner. The circumstances of the third (or working) group of the war invalids were also improved: the rule which became effective on May 1, 1965, stipulated that they could not be paid less than the established minimum disability pension. Steps were also taken to increase the temporary disability benefits.

A most important legislative act in the sphere of social security is the Law on Pensions and Allowances to Members of Collective Farms adopted on July 15, 1964, by the Fourth Session of the Sixth Supreme Soviet of the U.S.S.R. The Law said: "The possibility has now arisen of instituting a more stable system of social security at collective farms through a pension scheme covering old age and disability pensions, pensions in the event of death of the bread-winner, and also pregnancy and maternity allowances for women collective farmers.... The establishment of a state system of social security for collective farmers is another powerful incentive for stepping up the productive activity of collective farmers and increasing the output of farm produce.

"With the growth of the national income and, in particular, with the growth of the incomes of the collective farms, the pensions envisaged in the present Law shall be gradually increased to the level of the state pensions for factory, office and other workers."

In 1965, 6,800,000 collective farmers were already receiving pensions and benefits under this Law. More than that, after the Council of Ministers of the U.S.S.R. had on April 1, 1965, adopted its resolution on the Law on Pensions and Allowances to Members of Collective Farms, eligibility for pensions was also extended to the former members of those collective farms whose land had been turned over to state farms or other enterprises and organisations. And so, at the present time all aged and disabled collective farmers enjoy the benefits of social security on the basis of the principles and norms established by law, and receive their pensions from the centralised Union fund of collective farmers' social security.

Maternity and childbirth leave of 112 days, regardless of the length of the woman's work record on the collective farm, is now granted. The 56 post-natal leave is extended to 70 days in the event of complicated delivery or the birth of twins and more. Allowances are paid according to the same rules and norms as in the case of women industrial and office workers.

Pensions and benefits are provided from collective-farm and state funds, with no deductions made whatsoever from the earnings of the farmers themselves. As in the case of industrial and office workers, the collective farmers' pensions are not taxable.

A centralised Union fund of social security for collective farmers has been formed from which to pay the pensions and benefits set down by the new law. The State Budget of the U.S.S.R. allocates 400 million rubles a year for the purpose, and all collective farms contribute a share of their profits to this fund. In 1964, each collective farm paid in 2.5 per cent of its gross profits, and in 1965—4 per cent.

The Soviet plan of economic development for 1966-1970 envisages further pension benefits for employees and collective farmers, such as raising the minimum rate of old-age pensions, reducing the required seniority qualifications in the case of certain categories of workers, and extending to collective farmers a number of pension rules presently applicable to industrial and office workers.

Strengthening Legality

In the last few years, the Supreme Soviet of the U.S.S.R. and the Supreme Soviets of the Union Republics, following the extension of the legislative powers of the Union Republics, have adopted various enactments on civil and criminal law, the judicial system and judicial procedure, in order to strengthen socialist legality, consolidate citizens' constitutional rights, improve the democratic principles underlying the administration of justice, and bring the rules of law into conformity with the new conditions of social life.

In December 1961 the Supreme Soviet of the U.S.S.R. adopted the Fundamentals of Civil Legislation of the U.S.S.R. and the Union Republics, which set out the rules regulating property relations and some non-property relations in socialist society. These rules help to make effective use of the economic laws of socialism, further develop the socialist economy, raise the Soviet people's living standards, strengthen legality in the sphere of property relations and protection of the rights of socialist organisations and citizens. They help to consolidate the socialist economic system and socialist property, and to develop its various forms as they converge into one communist property. They also contribute to the tightening up of planning, contractual discipline, and economic accounting, boosting of Soviet trade, providing protection for the material and cultural interests of citizens, etc.

An important provision in the Fundamentals is that civil rights are subject to the protection of the law, except when they are used contrary to the interests of society. In the exercise of their rights and the fulfilment of their duties, citizens and organisations must observe the laws, respect the rules of the socialist way of life, and the moral principles of the society building communism.

The Fundamentals deal in great detail with the regulation of property relations involving citizens. The Fundamentals lay down the rule that only property intended to satisfy citizens' requirements may be in their personal ownership; it may not be used to derive unearned income. This should help to do away with the vestiges of bourgeois ideas, ethics and private-property attitudes among some citizens.

The Fundamentals give wider protection in civil law to personal non-property rights which arise from the citizens' use of public consumption funds, and the satisfaction of their material and cultural requirements by socialist organisations (purchase of household effects and consumer goods, use of housing, means of communication, transport, public utilities, services, etc.).

The Fundamentals of Civil Procedure of the U.S.S.R. and the Union Republics, adopted in December 1961, define the basic rights and duties of participants in civil proceedings, and the procedure in civil cases. The Fundamentals formulate the tasks of civil procedure: correct and expeditious adjudication of civil cases for the purpose of safeguarding the social and state system of the U.S.S.R., the socialist system of economy and socialist property; protection of the political, labour, housing and other personal and property rights and lawful interests of citizens, and also the rights and lawful interests of state establishments, enterprises, collective farms and other co-operative and mass organisations.

The Fundamentals establish that:

any party in interest has the right to invoke the court for protection of an infringed or contested right or lawful interest;

the court alone administers justice in civil cases; all citizens. irrespective of their social, property and official status, national and racial origin and religious beliefs are equal before the law and the court;

civil cases in all courts are tried by judges and people's assessors elected in the manner established by law;

cases in all courts are, as a rule, heard in public;

representatives of mass organisations and collectives of working people may take part in judicial proceedings to submit to the court the opinion of these organisations and collectives on the case before the court.

In accordance with the Fundamentals of Civil Legislation and the Fundamentals of Civil Procedure, the Union Republics have adopted new civil codes and codes of civil procedure.

The basic provisions, constituting the foundation of Soviet criminal legislation, are contained in the Fundamentals of Criminal Legislation of the U.S.S.R. and the Union Republics, which the Supreme Soviet of the U.S.S.R. approved on December 25, 1958.

The rules of the Fundamentals of Criminal Legislation, as of all other Soviet criminal laws, are informed with the ideas of true socialist humanism, and are designed to ensure the main tasks of criminal legislation, as defined by the Fundamentals: to provide protection for the Soviet social and constitutional system, socialist property, the person and the rights of citizens, and socialist law and order as a whole against criminal infringements.

The Fundamentals of Criminal Legislation clearly indicate the directions in which all-Union and republican legislation is to develop at the present stage. The humane character of Soviet criminal law is evident from the fact that it gives, on the one hand, severe treatment to malicious criminals and, on the other, repudiates cruelty, and holds out every chance of a fresh start for those who err or commit criminal offences through the force of circumstances.

What stands out in the Fundamentals of Criminal Legislation is the guarantee of legality in the institution of criminal proceedings and the application of punishment, which means that only persons guilty of committing a socially dangerous offence, as provided for in the criminal law, are subject to criminal prosecution and punishment. Criminal punishment may be imposed only by a sentence of the court. A prominent feature of the Fundamentals is that they open up real possibilities for the re-education of persons suffering criminal punishment and their return to honest labour as full-fledged citizens.

At the same time, the Supreme Soviet of the U.S.S.R. adopted a Law on Criminal Responsibility for Crimes Against the State, and a Law on Criminal Responsibility for Military Crimes.

All-Union criminal legislation was taken a step further when the Presidium of the Supreme Soviet of the U.S.S.R. enacted decrees aimed mainly at increasing responsibility for some crimes. Of great importance in the further strengthening of socialist legality and the legislative activity of the U.S.S.R. and the Union Republics in the maintenance of law and order were the July 1966 decisions of the Central Committee of the C.P.S.U., the Presidium of the Supreme Soviet of the U.S.S.R., and the Council of Ministers of the U.S.S.R. on measures to intensify the combating of offences against law and order, and also the decrees of the Presidium of the Supreme Soviet of the U.S.S.R., adopted on July 26, 1966, on Increasing Responsibility for Hooliganism and on Administrative Supervision by Organs of the Militia over Persons Released from Detention.

On December 25, 1958, the Supreme Soviet of the U.S.S.R. enacted the Fundamentals of Criminal Procedure of the U.S.S.R. and the Union Republics.

The Fundamentals say that the tasks of criminal procedure are speedy and full detection of crime, the bringing of the guilty to justice, correct application of the law to ensure that every offender suffers just punishment, and that no innocent person is prosecuted or convicted. Criminal procedure must help to strengthen socialist legality, prevent and eradicate crime, educate citizens in a spirit of undeviating observance of Soviet laws and respect for the rules of the socialist way of life.

The Fundamentals bind the court, the procurator, the investigator and the organs of inquiry, wherever the elements of crime come to light, to take all statutory measures to establish the corpus delicti of the crime, identify the guilty persons and punish them.

The Fundamentals contain firm guarantees of legality in criminal proceedings.

Supervision over the precise observance of the law in criminal procedure is exercised by the Procurator-General of the U.S.S.R. either directly or through subordinate procurators. It is the duty of the procurator at every stage of criminal proceedings to take timely statutory measures to cut short any infringements of the law, regardless of the source.

The Ordinance on the Supervisory Powers of the Procurator's Office in the U.S.S.R. was enacted by a decree of the Presidium of the U.S.S.R. Supreme Soviet of May 24, 1955.

Supervision over the precise observance of the laws in the Armed Forces of the U.S.S.R. is exercised by the Procurator-General of the U.S.S.R. and subordinate military procurators. The military procurator's office is given guidance by the Procurator-General of the U.S.S.R. either directly or through the Chief Military Procurator.

The Statute of the Military Procurator's Office was enacted by a Decree of the Presidium of the U.S.S.R. Supreme Soviet on December 14, 1966.

The Fundamentals of Legislation on the Judicial System of the U.S.S.R., and the Union and Autonomous Republics were promulgated by the Supreme Soviet of the U.S.S.R. on December 25, 1958. These Fundamentals describe the structure of the courts, the principles on which they operate, and their tasks. They state that in the U.S.S.R. justice is administered through the adjudication of civil and criminal cases by the courts.

The entire judiciary is elective, and all cases are examined in the courts collectively. In the administration of justice, judges and people's assessors are independent, and are subject only to the law.

Most courts—district (city) people's courts—are elected directly by the population. Other courts are elected by Soviets of Working People's Deputies.

To ensure the exercise of the right to defence in court—a right held out by Article 111 of the Constitution of the U.S.S.R.—and to extend other types of legal aid to citizens, enterprises, institutions and organisations, the Fundamentals provide for the establishment of a Collegium of Advocates, a voluntary association of persons engaged in legal advocacy. The Statute of the Collegium of Advocates in each Union Republic is approved by its Supreme Soviet.

The Supreme Court of the U.S.S.R. is the highest judicial body in the Soviet Union. The Statute of the Supreme Court of the U.S.S.R. was adopted by the Supreme Soviet of the U.S.S.R. on February 12, 1957.

In accordance with the Constitution of the U.S.S.R., the Supreme Court of the U.S.S.R. exercises supervision over the activity of the judicial bodies of the U.S.S.R., and the judicial bodies of the Union Republics, within the limits laid down by the Statute of the Supreme Court of the U.S.S.R.

The Supreme Court of the U.S.S.R., consisting of the chairman, deputy chairmen, members, and people's assessors, is elected by the Supreme Soviet of the U.S.S.R. for a term of five years. The composition of the Supreme Court of the U.S.S.R. reflects the federal character of the Soviet state and shows how the interests of the Union Republics are directly represented in the Union's highest judicial body: alongside the members of the Supreme Court who are elected by the Supreme Soviet, the chairmen of the Supreme Courts of the Union Republics are *ex officio* members of the Supreme Court of the U.S.S.R.

On December 25, 1958, the Supreme Soviet of the U.S.S.R. approved the Statute of the Military Tribunals, which are courts of the U.S.S.R., and are part of the single judicial system of the U.S.S.R. The main task of the military tribunals is to combat encroachments on the security of the U.S.S.R., consolidating the fighting capacity of its Armed Forces, military discipline and the procedures governing military service in the Armed Forces of the U.S.S.R.

Legislative Powers
of the Union Republics Extended

The Soviet legislative system consists of all-Union legislation and republican legislation. Under the Constitution of the U.S.S.R., the Supreme Soviets of the Union Republics were not empowered to legislate on civil law, criminal law, the judicial system or judicial procedure. In February 1957 the Supreme Soviet of the U.S.S.R. adopted a law conferring on the Union Republics powers to legislate on their judicial system, judicial procedure and civil and criminal codes, leaving the U.S.S.R. to legislate on the fundamentals of the judicial system and judicial procedure, and the fundamentals of civil and criminal law. This inaugurated a new stage in the codification of Soviet legislation.

In practice, this extension of the legislative powers of the Union Republics meant, for instance, that, apart from establishing responsibility for state and military crimes, which falls within the jurisdiction of the U.S.S.R., the Union Republics were free to specify, in their codes, all the concrete types of crimes and the penalties they carried.

The new codification of Soviet legislation has given rise to new democratic relationships between the legislative organs of the Union and its constituent Republics. As the latter framed their criminal and civil codes and other republican laws which were to be adopted under the new distribution of legislative powers between the Union and its constituent Republics, there arose the need to bring these republican laws into line with all-Union legislation, as the Constitution of the U.S.S.R. requires. At the same time, the legislative bodies of each Union Republic drew on the legislative experience of the other Union Republics, and this led to inter-republican scientific conferences on codification of law in the Union Republics. The Presidiums of the Supreme Soviets of the Union Republics also took some steps to co-ordinate the drafting of republican bills, thereby obtaining wider opportunities for drawing on the experience of bodies combating crime, and applying the achievements of Soviet juridical science.

Accordingly, as of February 1959, the Presidium of the Supreme Soviet of the U.S.S.R., at the request of the Presidiums of the Supreme Soviets of the Union Republics, organised consultations for lawyers engaged in the Union Republics on the framing of bills on the judicial system, the criminal and civil codes, the codes of criminal procedure, the codes of civil procedure, and other republican laws. This work was carried on with the participation of academic lawyers and officials of the Supreme Court, the Procurator's Office, the Juridical Commission under the Council of Ministers of the U.S.S.R. and other central departments in any way concerned with the bills in question. A consultative group worked out recommendations on each bill, and each relevant principle and conformity of bills with all-Union legislation were repeatedly discussed by the Presidium of the Supreme Soviet of the U.S.S.R. In some instances the Presidium of the Supreme Soviet of the U.S.S.R. also consulted the Committees for Legislative Proposals of the two chambers of the Supreme Soviet of the U.S.S.R.

For Lasting Peace
and International Co-operation

Much of the work done by the highest organ of state power in the U.S.S.R. is aimed at achieving mutual understanding between countries, at easing international tension, cementing friendship and developing co-operation between nations, and strengthening world peace.

It was precisely these considerations that prompted the Fourth Supreme Soviet of the U.S.S.R. to adopt on February 9, 1955, a Declaration addressed to all nations and world parliaments.

The Supreme Soviet of the U.S.S.R. drew the other parliaments' attention to the situation building up in Europe, Asia and other parts of the world which threatened the security of nations, and warned them that the imperialists were secretly preparing an atomic war. On behalf of the peoples of the Soviet Union, the Soviet Parliament stated that it thought it a matter of paramount importance to

The President of the Presidium of the Supreme Soviet of the U.S.S.R.
N. Podgorny shaking hands with Fiat workers in Turin on January
26, 1967, while on the state visit to Italy

have the relations between countries, big and small, based on such
international principles which would guarantee the development
of co-operation between nations in conditions of peace, i.e., on
principles of equality, non-interference in internal affairs, non-
aggression and non-encroachment on the territorial integrity
of other countries, and respect for sovereignty and national independence.

This Declaration which stated the basic principles of the Soviet
Union's peaceful foreign policy and also expressed the views of the
Soviet Government on the more important international issues, was
met with approval in many countries.

On July 16, 1956, the Fourth Supreme Soviet of the U.S.S.R.
adopted an Appeal to the parliaments of all countries in the world
for disarmament, in which it drew the attention of all nations, governments and parliaments to the crucial problem of the day—the
problem of stopping the arms race, of reducing armaments and banning atomic and nuclear weapons. The Appeal said that before May 1,
1957, the U.S.S.R. would make a further and bigger reduction in
its armed forces and a cut in the allocations for defence. The Supreme Soviet called upon the other parliaments to support the Soviet
initiative and by so doing make a worthy contribution to the cause
of world peace.

In the statement adopted by the Supreme Soviet of the U.S.S.R. that same day in connection with the Japanese Diet's appeal for banning nuclear weapons and also their tests, the solidarity of views existing between the Japanese and Soviet peoples on this problem was noted, and hope was expressed that its positive solution would be supported by the parliaments of the other countries.

The Soviet Government, pursuing the Leninist policy of peaceful coexistence of states with a different social system and anxious to help normalise the international situation, adopted a series of practical measures in the subsequent years for improving relations with the United States, Britain, France and other countries, and in 1959 placed before the United Nations its proposal for general and complete disarmament. The proposal envisaged the disbandment of all armed forces within the next four or five years, the scrapping of all armaments, the cessation of arms production, and the banning of all nuclear, chemical, bacteriological and rocket weapons.

Developing this peaceful initiative of the Council of Ministers of the U.S.S.R., the Fifth Supreme Soviet adopted on October 31, 1959, an Appeal to the parliaments of all the countries in the world, warning them of the danger of continuing the arms race which was drawing mankind into the holocaust of another war, and saying that parliaments, governments and statesmen should persistently seek ways of settling international issues, and in the first place the most burning problem of the day—that of disarmament. The road to eternal peace would be opened before mankind once these problems were settled, the Appeal said.

The Supreme Soviet of the U.S.S.R. heard the reports of the Soviet Government on measures taken to end nuclear weapon tests in the U.S.S.R. and adopted decisions on this question. Such decisions were, for instance, adopted on July 16, 1956, and May 10, 1957, at the Fifth and Seventh sessions respectively of the Fourth Supreme Soviet.

The deputies of the Supreme Soviet of the U.S.S.R., assembled on November 6, 1957, for a jubilee session to mark the fortieth anniversary of the Soviet state, appealled to all nations, all workers and peasants, all workers in science and culture, political and public leaders, parliaments and governments of all the countries in the world to fight for peaceful coexistence of states with a different social system, for general disarmament, for the banning of nuclear weapons and the cessation of tests, for a system of collective security, and for international co-operation.

The Supreme Soviet of the U.S.S.R. making a new contribution to the cause of strengthening peace and creating an atmosphere of trust between nations, in its decision of December 21, 1957, instructed the Soviet Government to explore the possibility of further reducing the Armed Forces of the Soviet Union provided, of course, that this would not be detrimental to the interests of the state's defence. The supreme organ of Soviet state power expressed the hope that the United States, Great Britain and France would follow suit and thereby facilitate the achievement of genuine international security.

In March 1958, the Supreme Soviet of the U.S.S.R. adopted a decision on the Soviet Union's unilateral cessation of atomic and hydrogen tests. At the same time the Supreme Soviet called on the parliaments of other countries to do everything necessary to end nuclear weapon tests there, and instructed the Council of Ministers of the U.S.S.R. to address an appeal to the governments of nuclear powers, urging them to take measures ensuring the cessation of atomic and hydrogen bomb tests for ever.

At the same session, on March 31, 1958, the Supreme Soviet of the U.S.S.R. addressed an appeal to the United States Congress, to the Parliament of Great Britain, to the parliaments of all countries in the world, and a special appeal to the Bundestag of the Federal Republic of Germany. These documents expressed the hope that the parliaments of these and other countries would use their influence to ban nuclear weapon tests for all time, that this question would at last be definitely settled as the whole world hopes it would, and that the Bundestag of the Federal Republic of Germany would speak out against the atomic arming of West Germany and any attempts to involve it in dangerous adventures.

Furthermore, on instructions from the Supreme Soviet of the U.S.S.R. the representatives of the two chambers addressed the parliaments of states—members of the anti-Hitlerite coalition and countries which had suffered from nazi aggression during the Second World War—with a call to unite their efforts in preventing the arming of the Federal Republic of Germany with rockets and atomic bombs.

These appeals were made known to the parliaments of the foreign countries concerned, and were another proof of the Soviet Parliament's constant concern for the strengthening of international security.

Controlling the foreign policy activity of the Council of Ministers of the U.S.S.R. and taking account of the importance of international issues, the Supreme Soviet of the U.S.S.R. heard and discussed at regular intervals the Council's reports. At the First and Sixth sessions of the fifth convocation, and also at the First Session of the sixth convocation it was the Minister of Foreign Affairs of the U.S.S.R. who made these reports and statements; at the Third and Fourth sessions of the fifth convocation and at the Second Session of the sixth convocation it was the Chairman of the Council of Ministers of the U.S.S.R.

These reports elucidated the international situation, characterised the foreign policy activity of the leading capitalist powers, named the cardinal international problems, indicated ways of settling them, and stated in detail the stand of the Soviet Government on different international issues, a stand that invariably helped to improve the relations between states. The Soviet Government reiterated again and again that the problems facing the world could be settled only if all the states showed good will and only if they acted not from positions of strength but from positions of common sense.

Discussing the foreign policy of the Soviet Government at sessions of the Supreme Soviet of the U.S.S.R. the deputies emphasised the fact that it did not merely answer the vital interests of the Soviet Union but also the interests of all peace-loving countries, and was, therefore, fully approved by the Soviet people and their nominees to this highest legislative body. After keen discussions of the foreign policy pursued by the Council of Ministers of the U.S.S.R. the Supreme Soviet invariably adopted unanimous resolutions fully approving it.

At the First Session of the Seventh Supreme Soviet the head of the newly formed Government of the U.S.S.R. A. Kosygin made a statement on August 3, 1966, on the cardinal questions of the Soviet Union's home and foreign policy.

The Supreme Soviet approved the main directions of the Government's activity in the sphere of home and foreign policy as outlined in the statement.

Assuming an active role in Soviet foreign policy undertakings, the Supreme Soviet itself made peace-promoting proposals to foreign parliaments and also voiced its attitude to statements made by parliaments of other countries aimed at strengthening world peace.

On April 29, 1965, the chairmen of the two chambers of the Supreme Soviet sent the National Assembly of the Democratic Republic of Vietnam a reply to their appeal to the parliaments of other states for a peaceful normalisation of the situation in their country.

"The Supreme Soviet of the U.S.S.R. fully supports the Appeal of the National Assembly of the Democratic Republic of Vietnam to the parliaments of different countries in the world, and wholly approves of the proposals contained therein, aimed at a peaceful normalisation of the situation in Vietnam," the reply said in part. The Supreme Soviet stated that the aggravation of the situation in Vietnam and elsewhere in Southeast Asia was caused solely by the aggressive policy of the American imperialists, which was threatening the security of nations not just in that region but everywhere in the world. The reply further stated that the criminal actions of the American military in Vietnam were wrathfully condemned by all Soviet people. The way to restore peace in that part of the world was for the U.S.A. to revert to the Geneva Agreements on Vietnam signed in 1954.

The Supreme Soviet of the U.S.S.R. called on foreign parliaments to support the Appeal of the National Assembly of the Democratic Republic of Vietnam.

In view of the escalation of the American aggression in Vietnam which is causing increasing international tension and is creating a serious threat to peace and the security of all nations and states, the supreme body of power in the U.S.S.R. returned on several occasions to the discussion of the situation in Indo-China.

On August 3, 1966, at its first session, the Seventh Supreme Soviet of the U.S.S.R. adopted a statement in connection with the increasing aggression of U.S. imperialism in Vietnam. Once again, it resolutely condemned the imperialist aggression in Vietnam, and stated that the whole weight of the responsibility for the continuation and the escalation of this criminal war together with the ensuing consequences falls on the Government of the United States.

On behalf of the Soviet population of 234,000,000, the Supreme Soviet announced that the Soviet Union would do everything within its power to help the heroic Vietnamese in their struggle for independence and freedom.

The Supreme Soviet called on all governments and parliaments to come out in defence of the principles of justice and law in international relations.

In its afore-mentioned undertakings the Supreme Soviet was guided by its concern for the security and welfare of nations. Peace, freedom, independence and co-operation between nations—such are the aims which determine its foreign policy.

Everyone knows that in order to achieve these noble aims all states must act in accord. However, many of the concrete proposals made by the Soviet Union and its highest legislative body, aimed at easing international tension and strengthening the security of nations, were unfortunately left unachieved. The parliaments and governments of many capitalist powers failed to justify the peoples' hopes and did not make a worthy contribution to the honourable cause of peace. Not only did they refuse to support many of the Soviet peace proposals, but sometimes they actually hindered their realisation.

This refers to such important matters as the Soviet Union's proposal on general and complete disarmament, on banning atomic and hydrogen weapons, on preventing the rocket and nuclear arming of the Federal Republic of Germany, and others.

At the same time special mention must be made of the fact that the Supreme Soviet's peace proposals were always warmly supported by the supreme legislative bodies of the socialist states which themselves made more than one constructive proposal, the adoption of which would have strengthened world peace.

Exchange of Parliamentary Delegations

The present international situation requires the states and their parliaments to double their efforts to develop mutual understanding and friendly co-operation between nations, and strengthen universal peace and security. The Supreme Soviet of the U.S.S.R. pointed to this need already in February 1955 in its Declaration addressed to all the world's nations and parliaments.

Nations are vitally interested in stabilising universal peace, the Declaration said. It is possible for them to avert another war because the forces of peace are steadily growing and are already now more powerful than the forces of aggression and war. Considering that the responsibility for preserving and strengthening peace rests with parliaments, since it is they who pass the laws on war and peace, the Supreme Soviet of the U.S.S.R. pointed out in its Declaration that establishing direct contacts between parliaments, exchanging parliamentary delegations, and having members of these delegations speak in each other's parliaments would promote the principles of international co-operation, and would meet the peoples' desire for friendlier relations.

The development of the Supreme Soviet's international ties was a direct result of the Declaration which evoked a positive response from many nations and parliaments. Since the adoption of the Declaration, the Supreme Soviet's parliamentary connections with foreign countries were considerably broadened to include an exchange of parliamentary delegations, mutual visits of parliamentary leaders, visits to the Soviet Union by individual foreign members of parliament or groups of members, exchange of messages, greetings, and so on.

Prior to the adoption of the Declaration on February 9, 1955, only two parliamentary delegations (from Great Britain and Finland, in 1954) came to the Soviet Union at the invitation of the Supreme Soviet; since 1955 such visits have been regular.

The following countries have since sent their parliamentary delegations to the Soviet Union:

Albania, Austria, Belgium, France, India, Iran, Japan, Luxemburg, Poland, Sweden, Syria, Yugoslavia (1955);

Brazil, Bulgaria, the Chinese People's Republic, Czechoslovakia, the Democratic Repubic of Vietnam, Denmark, the German Democratic Republic, Greece, Hungary, Indonesia, the Korean People's Democratic Republic, Norway, Pakistan, Rumania, Uruguay (1956);

Burma (1957);

Cambodia, Iceland, the Mongolian People's Republic, the Sudan, Thailand (1958);

Afghanistan, Guinea (1959);

Bolivia, Chile, Costa Rica, Ghana, Mexico, Nepal (1960);

Bolivia, Brazil, Cyprus, Japan, Libya, Peru, the United Arab Republic, Venezuela (1961);

Afghanistan, Ceylon, Czechoslovakia, Hungary, India, Kenya, Mali, Poland, Togo, Yugoslavia (1962);

Brazil, Bulgaria, Colombia, Congo (Kinshasa), Costa Rica, Indonesia, Mexico, Nigeria, Rumania, Sierra Leone, Somalia, Tunisia, Turkey (1963);

Burundi, Congo (Brazzaville), Japan, the Mongolian People's Republic, Pakistan (1964);

Canada, Chile, Costa Rica, Dagomey, the Democratic Republic of Vietnam, the Lebanon, Somalia (1965);

Austria, the German Democratic Republic, Hungary, Iran, Mali, Nepal, Rumania, Sweden, Turkey, Yugoslavia, Zambia (1966).

Ethiopia, the United Arab Republic (1967).

Parliamentary delegations from Afghanistan, Austria, Bolivia, Bulgaria, Chile, Czechoslovakia, the Democratic Republic of Vietnam, the German Democratic Republic, India, Indonesia, Iran, Mali, Mexico, the Mongolian People's Republic, Nepal, Pakistan, Poland, Somalia, Sweden, Turkey, and the United Arab Republic came to the Soviet Union twice, and delegations from Brazil, Costa Rica, Hungary, Japan, Rumania and Yugoslavia three times.

In other words, from February 1955, when the Declaration was adopted by the Supreme Soviet of the U.S.S.R., to mid-1967 the Soviet Union was visited by 97 official parliamentary delegations from 64 countries.

Among the delegates there were representatives of influential political parties and parliamentary groups and non-party people of different social and official standing: state and public figures, ministers, members of standing parliamentary committees, mayors, bankers, businessmen, landholders, scientists, trade union leaders, teachers, lawyers, workers, peasants, members of agricultural co-operatives—in short, people of different political views and religions, each with their own attitude to the Soviet system and each with their own evaluation of Soviet reality.

Foreign guests met and spoke with the chairmen of the chambers and the deputies of the Supreme Soviet of the U.S.S.R., the Supreme Soviets of Union and Autonomous Republics, the local Soviets, as well as with heads and officials of ministries and departments, trade unions and co-operatives, with workers, collective farmers, scientists, industrial and agricultural specialists, and people in science, art and culture. Many of the delegates were received by the leaders of the Communist Party and the Soviet Government and had long talks with them.

The parliamentary delegations from Iran, Poland, Ghana, Mexico, Kenya and Turkey, who came to the Soviet Union when the Supreme Soviet of the U.S.S.R. was in session, attended sittings of the two chambers. The heads of the delegations from Iran, Poland and Turkey made speeches at the joint sittings of the Soviet of the Union and the Soviet of Nationalities.

The leader of Turkey's parliamentary delegation, Chairman of the National Chamber Ferouk Bosbeili, said in his speech at the First Session of the Seventh Supreme Soviet on August 3, 1966, that the main concern of mankind was peace, the defence of peace, and the preservation of peace. People realise that for a better life on earth, for greater prosperity, and the guarantee of a secure future for the coming generations it is imperative to preserve peace. "The visit of our parliamentary delegation to the Soviet Union in 1963 proved to be an important factor in the development of Turko-Soviet relations. And we trust that this present visit of ours will also be a new step forward," Ferouk Bosbeili said. "We can see how splendidly the parliaments of both our countries perform their duties in the matter of developing mutual relations. . . . We are especially gratified when we see that people are working towards this end at all levels."

Ferouk Bosbeili's speech was well received by the deputies of the Supreme Soviet.

Visits to the Soviet Union and acquaintance with the Soviet Government's home and foreign policies, with Soviet democracy and Soviet achievements, enables the foreign parliamentary delegates to gain a better understanding of what is happening in this country, to see for themselves the falsity of the numerous stories spread by reactionary propaganda about Soviet reality, to witness the peaceful, creative work of the Soviet people and to convince themselves of their desire to live in peace and friendship with the peoples of other countries.

Visits by Supreme Soviet delegations at the invitation of foreign parliaments, also play an important role in developing co-operation between nations and establishing direct contacts between parliaments and members of parliament.

Supreme Soviet delegations visited 50 foreign countries in the 13 years from 1954 to mid-1967.

In 1954, they went to Finland;

In 1955, to Albania, Bulgaria, Czechoslovakia, the German Democratic Republic, Hungary, Poland and Yugoslavia;

In 1956, to Austria, Belgium, Britain, Luxemburg, Rumania, Sweden and Syria;

In 1957, to the Chinese People's Republic, the Democratic Republic of Vietnam, Iran, the Korean People's Democratic Republic, and the Mongolian People's Republic;

In 1958, to Burma, India, Pakistan and Uruguay;

In 1959, to Indonesia;

In 1960, to Bolivia, Denmark, Guinea, Iceland, Mexico, Norway and Poland;

In 1961, to Afghanistan, Chile, Czechoslovakia and Hungary;

In 1962, to Bolivia and Rumania;

In 1963, to Bulgaria, Ghana, the Democratic Republic of Vietnam, Mali and Yugoslavia;

In 1964, to Greece, India, Indonesia, France, Japan, Mexico, the Mongolian People's Republic, Nigeria, Somalia and the United Arab Republic;

In 1965, to Congo (Brazzaville), Hungary, Sierra Leone and Turkey;

In 1966, to Britain, Cambodia, Canada, Chile, Ethiopia, Libya and Pakistan;

In 1967, to Czechoslovakia, the Lebanon, Mali and Zambia.

Supreme Soviet delegations made two official visits to Bolivia, Britain, Bulgaria, Chile, the Democratic Republic of Vietnam, India, Indonesia, Mali, Mexico, the Mongolian People's Republic, Pakistan, Poland, Rumania and Yugoslavia and three visits to Czechoslovakia and Hungary.

These Soviet parliamentary delegations were offered an opportunity to acquaint themselves with the economic and cultural achievements in these countries. Members of the delegations met high-standing government officials, people working in science, culture and art, workers, peasants and intellectuals.

The foreign trips of the Supreme Soviet delegations are becoming important political events in the countries they visit, giving the representatives of parliamentary, government and business circles a chance to discuss problems of interest to both sides, drawing the attention of public opinion to problems of co-operation between nations and prompting a more active development of relations between them and thus contributing to world peace.

Before many parliamentary delegations had exchanged visits, it became obvious that new, important avenues in the matter of establishing co-operation between nations and strengthening international security had been found.

The Supreme Soviet of the U.S.S.R., when reviewing questions of foreign policy, stressed on more than one occasion the importance of these exchanges. "Another fact responsible for easing the international situation," the Supreme Soviet Decision dated August 5, 1955, said, "is the establishment of direct contacts between parliaments and the exchange of parliamentary delegations, started on the initiative of the Supreme Soviet of the U.S.S.R."

This question of exchanges was put on the agenda of the Fourth Session of the Fourth Supreme Soviet. The deputies who took the floor expressed a positive opinion of the reciprocal visits of Supreme Soviet delegations and foreign parliament representatives, for they enable the visiting party to make a more thorough acquaintance with the state system, economy, culture and life of the countries they visit.

The Decision adopted by the Supreme Soviet of the U.S.S.R. on this question said: "The Supreme Soviet of the U.S.S.R believes that the exchange of parliamentary delegations, just as the development of other forms of parliamentary contacts, will help to further the mutual understanding of nations and consequently will have a beneficial influence on easing international tension, on safeguarding and strengthening world peace.

"The Supreme Soviet of the U.S.S.R. declares that efforts on the part of parliaments to develop links and contacts in the interests of international co-operation and greater mutual trust between countries, will in future have the warm sympathy and full support of the Supreme Soviet of the U.S.S.R. and all Soviet people."

One of the most vivid manifestations of the democratic character of Soviet power is the participation of the people in the making of laws. Every law passed by the Supreme Soviet of the U.S.S.R. is in effect an expression of the people's will, the result of the deputies' collective endeavour in weighing up the diverse and sometimes conflicting points of view, in studying thousands of proposals coming from the working people in their letters, and in deliberating the opinions of the electorate, the government and non-government organisations, and the republican and local organs of state power. As a rule, bills are discussed on a nation-wide scale before they are considered by the Supreme Soviet.

These bills are published in the central press, in *Izvestia, Pravda, Trud* and a number of other Russian-language mass circulation newspapers, and also in the newspapers of the Union and Autonomous Republics which come out in the languages spoken there. The entire population, therefore, is able to acquaint itself with the bills and think them over.

All the citizens of the Soviet Union keenly discussed such bills, published in the central press, as, for instance, the Bill on State Pensions (1956), and the Bill on Closer Links between School and Life and on further developing the system of public education (1958).

This popular discussion of questions which the Supreme Soviet of the U.S.S.R. has to deliberate and pass a decision on, comes from the high political awareness of citizens, from their concern for the development of their socialist state and its economy, from their desire to improve the laws for the common good.

The Twenty-Third Congress of the C.P.S.U. adopted the Directives for the five-year plan of economic development. These Directives, which had been published in the press and which incorporated the opinions and suggestions of millions—Party members and non-Party people—who had thoroughly discussed the target figures at their enterprises, collective and state farms, form the basis of the annual draft plans of economic development set before the Supreme Soviet of the U.S.S.R. by the Soviet Government.

The working people themselves participate in drawing up, discussing and implementing the draft plans of economic development. They also take a keen interest in bills aimed at raising the population's living standards. For instance, the Bill on State Pensions, drafted by the Council of Ministers of the U.S.S.R. and published in the central and local newspapers in 1956, was discussed practically in every family. The Legislative Proposals Committees of the Soviet of the Union and the Soviet of Nationalities received more than twelve thousand letters addressed directly to them, containing the citizens' comments and suggestions.

The discussion of this bill lasted two months, and during that time letters poured in a steady stream to the Supreme Soviet of the U.S.S.R., the Central Committee of the C.P.S.U., the Council of Ministers of the U.S.S.R. and the newspapers. All this mail was subsequently sent to the Legislative Proposals Committees. Not a single letter was passed over, and every suggestion, irrespective of who made it and in what form, was given due consideration.

As a result of this nation-wide discussion, the Bill on State Pensions was considerably improved, both in content and in wording.

Here is one suggestion which came from a group of women living in Donetsk:

"We beg the Committee for Legislative Proposals to give a mind to us, women, who do not only work in production but are also active members of the community. We bring up our children and do the housework, so we think that mothers of large families should be eligible for pension earlier, and not at 55 as proposed."

The Committees supported this suggestion, and the pension law stipulates that women who had given birth to and brought up five or more children to the age of eight are eligible for pension at fifty. Consideration was also given to the suggestion made in many of the letters received that a work record of thirty-five years should entitle a person to an increased pension.

In addition to the publication of main bills in the central press, another widespread practice is to publish those of a less general nature in special magazines and bulletins. The purpose is to invite a more through and efficient discussion, to draw into it the scientists and experts concerned, and to enable them to exchange their views on the pages of these magazines.

Published in February-March 1958 were drafts of such important legislative acts as the Fundamentals of Criminal Legislation and the Fundamentals of Criminal Procedure of the U.S.S.R. and the Union Republics; in July-August 1960—the draft Fundamentals of Civil Legislation and the Fundamentals of Civil Procedure of the U.S.S.R. and the Union Republics; Fundamentals of Labour Legislation and the Bill on Enhancing the Role of the Community in Combating Violations of Soviet Legality and the Rules of Socialist Community Life. The publications were made in the magazines *Soviety Deputatov Trudyashchikhsya, Sovietskoye Gosudarstvo i Pravo, Sovietskaya Yustitsia, Sotsialisticheskaya Zakonnost, Sovietskiye Profsoyuzy, Sotsialistichesky Trud, Voprosy Ekonomiki* and the bulletin *Byulleten Verkhovnogo Suda SSSR* as well as in some other periodicals. The total circulation of these magazines exceeds half a million copies.

Among those who discussed the above-mentioned draft laws there were officials from central bodies and local Soviets, from judicial bodies, procurators and lawyers, the militia, legal advisers, members of various mass organisations—trade unions, Komsomol and others—members of comrades' courts, and so on.

Problems connected with these bills were discussed at scientific conferences in Moscow, Leningrad, Kiev, Riga, Tbilisi, Tallinn and other large cities, with many prominent scholars and specialists taking active part. All their conclusions, comments and constructive proposals were then set before the Supreme Soviet of the U.S.S.R.

The magazines, in which these bills were published, regularly carried articles, notices and reports on the progress of discussions. For instance, in the eighteen months that the draft Fundamentals of Civil Legislation and the Fundamentals of Civil Procedure were under discussion, as many as 175 articles, not to mention other material, were published in *Sovietskoye Gosudarstvo i Pravo*, *Sotsialisticheskaya Zakonnost* and *Sovietskaya Yustitsia*, taking just these three specialised magazines. Roughly two thousand suggestions, comments and additions were addressed directly to the Committees for Legislative Proposals.

By drawing the population into discussion of these highly important normative acts, and by studying and adopting certain of the suggestions made, the Supreme Soviet was enabled to make some essential amendments and additions. Here are just a few of the additions made to the draft Fundamentals of Civil Legislation:

a preamble was drafted and later adopted by the Supreme Soviet stating the aims and tasks of Soviet civil legislation (suggested by the staff of the Institute of State and Law, Academy of Sciences of the U.S.S.R.);

an article on the protection of the Soviet citizens' honour and dignity was included in the Fundamentals (on numerous suggestions contained in letters from different people);

an article was also included stipulating that the exercise of civil rights and the execution of duties must not contradict socialist legality and socialist law and order (suggested by people employed in Kiev judiciary bodies).

Clauses were also added on suggestions made by workers in trade and supported by the Ministry of Trade of the R.S.F.S.R., regulating the sale of goods on credit, the hire of household appliances and the system of placing orders for their repair. These services had not as yet been very widespread when the bill was being drawn up, and the inclusion of a few clauses on the subject greatly helped their development.

The discussion and publication of the draft Fundamentals of Criminal Legislation and the draft Fundamentals of the Criminal Procedure of the U.S.S.R. and the Union Republics resulted in the introduction of more than thirty amendments and a large number of corrections for greater clarity.

The wishes of people, expressed in letters to the Committees for Legislative Proposals or to the press, and the comments of mass and scientific organisations influence the law-making process at all its stages. It is well known that the question of nature protection in the U.S.S.R., of the need to protect forests from indiscriminate felling and the rivers and lakes from pollution, to combat soil erosion and salinity, and so forth, was long and widely discussed. As a result of this campaign, in which many thousands of people living in different parts of the country took part, bills on the Land Use, on the exploitation of waters and mineral wealth were drawn up by the Supreme Soviet.

Work on drafting the Basic Principles of Forest Exploitation in the U.S.S.R. began with the decision adopted by the Presidium of the Supreme Soviet of the U.S.S.R. on July 9, 1965, which said that: "After studying the recommendations presented by the Academic Council of the Department of Forest Exploitation of the Kirov Academy of Forestry in Leningrad, and also by members of the Scientific and Technical Society of the Timber Industry and Forestry, the Presidium suggests that the Committees for Legislative Proposals of the Soviet of the Union and the Soviet of Nationalities should proceed to draw up the Basic Principles of Forest Exploitation."

The Soviet citizens' initiative and their anxiety to improve Soviet legislation are treated with great attention and care by the organs of state power. Their letters and suggestions are studied and summed up, the opinion of the majority is ascertained, and the more pressing problems calling for an urgent solution are given priority.

The broad discussion of the bills by the population is actually one of the final stages of the work. But even in its initial stages public opinion is reckoned with and the views of experienced, competent specialists are taken into account. As mentioned earlier, bills are first worked out by highly representative subcommittees, formed for the purpose by the standing committees of the Supreme Soviet's two chambers.

Every standing committee naturally has its own activists engaged in their particular field. For example, the Planning and Budgetary Committee draws economists, planners and finance experts into the elaboration of their bills; the Committees for Agriculture enlist the help of agriculturists, livestock experts, and builders specialising in collective-farm and state-farm construction. The main point is that all bills worked out by the Supreme Soviet absorb the opinions of the broad sections of the population and reflect the demands of the entire Soviet people.

The composition of the subcommittees depends to a large extent on the nature of the bill under discussion and in addition to deputies of the Supreme Soviet includes specialists in the pertinent branch of economy or culture and lawyers specialising in that branch of law.

Party, trade union, Komsomol and other mass organisations are also represented.

The composition of these subcommittees in 1965 was roughly as follows:

	Total number of members	Specialists and practical workers	Scientific workers	Representatives of mass organisations	Heads of ministries and departments	Managers of enterprises, organisations and establishments
Basic Principles of Land Use	31	10	8	3	5	5
Fundamentals of Matrimonial Law	32	11	9	4	5	3
Fundamentals of Legislation on Exploitation of Water Resources	50	19	10	6	9	6
Fundamentals of Legislation on Health Protection	44	17	12	6	5	4
Fundamentals of Corrective Labour Legislation	40	9	14	5	8	4
Basic Principles of the Exploitation of Mineral Wealth	28	11	8	3	3	3
Basic Principles of Forest Exploitation	40	12	15	3	5	5
Law on Accounting and Statistics	44	17	12	3	7	5

Suggestions coming from mass organisations and, therefore, expressing public opinion are considered with particular attention.

Before publishing the bills in the press, the Supreme Soviet's committees conduct polls, discussions and conferences with people in order to ascertain what public opinion has to say on the practical application of the laws on the Statute Books. By securing this information at the initial stage, the committees are able to reflect the demands of the population in the bills, and to correctly solve the tasks confronting legislation.

For example, after the appearance of a press notice that the Committees for Legislative Proposals had started work on the draft Fundamentals of Matrimonial Law, discussions were held on a wide scale to provisionally decide on the marriageable age, the terms and forms of registration, the rights of parenthood, and so on.

One such discussion was held in March 1963 at the Zasulauka Textile Mill in Riga in which four hundred women employees took part. The majority supported the proposals made by the committees and aimed at strengthening the ties of family and marriage. At the same time some suggestions were made to simplify divorce proceedings in cases where the marriage had definitely broken up with no hope of mending.

The suggestions voiced at this and other meetings were embodied in the Decree of the Presidium of the Supreme Soviet of the U.S.S.R., adopted on December 1965 and later endorsed by the Supreme Soviet on Certain Changes in Divorce Proceedings. In compliance with the wishes of the working people the two-stage court hearing was abolished, as was also the rule of publishing a preliminary notice in the newspaper.

Other clauses of the Matrimonial Law were also discussed. For example, the question of alimony for the maintenance of children, as regards amount and payment, was the point at issue at a meeting attended by 250 women employees at the Makhachkala Sewing Factory in Daghestan. All the concrete proposals made by the women who took the floor were thoroughly studied by the subcommittee concerned.

As a rule such meetings are conducted by members of standing committees or subcommittees arriving for the purpose from Moscow. Local Party and government organisations are always asked to help with the arrangement of these meetings, conferences and discussions. All the comments and suggestions voiced are summed up in order to elucidate the opinion of the majority. Every suggestion is considered by the subcommittee and a resolution passed on whether it is to be included in the bill, used in the later stages of work, or declined. Thus, not a single one of the proposals made in the course of discussion is disregarded.

More often than not, the proposals are amendments or repetitions of a drafted clause in a different wording. But not infrequently they raise points of principle, and the subcommittee has to devote several sittings to their examination.

This happened, for instance, when the draft Basic Principles of Land Use was discussed in 1964. The question of land use in populated rural areas came up. Should this land be treated apart from that occupied by the collective and state farms? What legal status should apply to this land and who should be in charge of it? These questions were brought up for discussion at the meetings of the committees themselves, and also at conferences with the local Soviet and Party officials, with the rural population of the Ukraine, Byelorussia, Uzbekistan, Georgia, Bashkiria, Voronezh and Omsk regions. The unanimous opinion was to have special clauses in the law governing the legal status of the land in populated rural areas and to have a provision made in the law guaranteeing the development and modernisation of the villages. Clauses to this effect were accordingly included in the bill.

The population does more than just offer suggestions, criticism and advice, it also provides information and material needed by the Supreme Soviet of the U.S.S.R. in its preparatory work on the bills. The committees, therefore, know how matters stand and exactly how the people feel about the questions which they are drawing up into a law. Without knowing the opinion of the workers and farmers and without having a complete picture of how the law is applied in practice, it would be impossible to decide such questions as the extent of an industrial enterprise's powers, the best way to combat the pollution of water sources, the limits of parenthood rights, and so on.

Materials of this nature are first of all supplied by the central departments—statistical boards, courts, procurators' offices, land departments, etc. Direct polls are also very helpful in elaborating the bills and eliciting the necessary information.

Thus, when the Fundamentals of Matrimonial Law were being drafted, citizens were directly consulted on whether a definite time limit should be set between the application for a marriage license and the marriage ceremony. The consensus of opinion was that it would be a good thing to introduce such a rule, since it would engender in the applicants a more serious attitude to the important step they were taking. For fuller information, Krasnoyarsk, Frunze and a number of other cities were polled, and all of them confirmed the correctness of the proposal made.

The preparatory work on the drafts of the Basic Principles of Land Use, Matrimonial Law, Exploitation of Water Resources and others, also made it necessary to consult the rural and urban population in different parts of the country: industrial workers, peasants, office workers, scientists, people working in culture and art, housewives, servicemen—in short, everybody whom the bills under discussion could concern.

In 1963-1965 separate clauses in the three above-mentioned bills were discussed at meetings and conferences in ten of the Union Republics, nine territories and regions of the R.S.F.S.R., among them such different ones as the Lithuanian S.S.R., the Krasnoyarsk Territory, Ivanovo Region and Tajikistan. The practice of drawing different geographical regions and all segments of society into discussion of the bills ensures a perfect elucidation of the Soviet citizens' views and allows a correct reflection to be made in these bills of the Union Republics' national, geographical and economic peculiarities.

As a result of such discussions, clauses are introduced which leave the decision on certain local questions to the legislatures of the Union Republics. To name a few instances, there was the question of allowing a younger marriageable age in exceptional cases, the stipulation of certain terms in purchase and sale contracts, the question of control over the correct use of land, and other points of a local character.

Soviet socialist society is intolerant towards drunkards, hooligans and other persons who violate public law and order. In their letters to the newspapers and to the Supreme Soviet of the U.S.S.R. the working people demanded that a more resolute struggle should be waged against hooliganism.

Heeding the demands of the community, the Presidium of the Supreme Soviet of the U.S.S.R. adopted a Decree on July 26, 1966, on Greater Criminal Responsibility for Hooliganism, and at their next session the deputies of the Supreme Soviet unanimously approved it.

The people's participation in the making of laws and their influence on the establishment of legal rules does not stop at the Supreme Soviet passing the law. Thus the Fourth Session of the Sixth Supreme Soviet (July 1964) formed a special committee to elaborate proposals on the system and size of deductions to be made from collective-farm incomes towards the all-Union fund of social security for farmers. The committee sent more than twenty representatives to different parts of the country (North Caucasus, the Ukraine, Moldavia, Central Russian regions, Central Asia, Siberia and the Baltic Republics) to make a sample survey of the collective farms and ascertain the views of the farmers on the size of the proposed deductions. The data and the proposals, received as a result of surveying some thirty collective farms and canvassing the opinion of a considerable number of farmers, made the basis of the decisions adopted by the Council of Ministers of the U.S.S.R.

The amendments and improvements of the laws in force proposed by the people are carried into effect. In 1965 the committees of the Supreme Soviet of the U.S.S.R. verified the implementation of the Law on Universal Eight-Year Schooling drawing into the work a large number of public education and local Soviet officials, and activists. It was noted that in many of the Union Republics, territories and regions little thought was given to the transport facilities for village children who had a very long way to go to school. The Presidium of the Supreme Soviet of the U.S.S.R. studied all the proposals made on this question and adopted a decision in which it instructed the Presidiums of the Supreme Soviets of the Union Republics to arrange free travel to and from primary, eight-year and ten-year schools for pupils resident in rural areas. Since September 1, 1965, all these children have been going to school fare free.

However correct it may be, the opinion of the population on the bills under discussion needs to be properly worded. In this the committees rely on the assistance of scientists. The most prominent Soviet scientists actively co-operate with the subcommittees in preparing, analysing and summing up the materials.

The Institutes of the Academy of Sciences of the U.S.S.R. and other research institutes and educational establishments arrange discussions, seminars and conferences on instructions from the standing committees or on their own initiative to analyse certain points in the bills from the angle of the latest scientific achievements. For example, the draft Fundamentals of Matrimonial Law and the Fundamentals of Corrective Labour Legislation were circulated among some thirty institutes and universities, and the draft Fundamentals of Health Protection Legislation was sent for discussion to fifty-eight medical colleges and law institutes.

The medical profession—academicians, professors and doctors, thousands of qualified staff members of hospitals in the fifteen Union Republics—expressed their view on the cardinal problems of further developing the health services and also on the more narrowly professional questions such as the introduction of an oath for graduating doctors, fare-free travel by any means of transport in case of need, etc.

. The Soviet Parliament reflects in all its activity the will and the interests of the Soviet people, using every form and method to draw the broadest sections of the population into the elaboration of Soviet laws.

PARLIAMENTARY GROUP OF THE U.S.S.R.

To give a comprehensive picture of the Supreme Soviet manifold activities, it is necessary to outline the work of its deputies in the Inter-Parliamentary Union.

The aims of the Inter-Parliamentary Union, it will be remembered, are to promote personal contacts among members of all parliaments constituted into National Groups and unite them in common action, with a view to strengthening and developing democratic institutions, as well as to advance work on behalf of peace and international collaboration. (Statutes of the Inter-Parliamentary Union, Art. 1.)

These aims could not but find support both of individual deputies and of the Supreme Soviet as a whole.

A conference attended by 133 deputies of the Fourth Supreme Soviet on June 29, 1955, passed a Decision on the Formation of a Parliamentary Group of the U.S.S.R. and Joining the Inter-Parliamentary Union. The decision stated that the deputies of the Supreme Soviet had studied the Statutes of the Inter-Parliamentary Union and the aims they proclaimed. Proceeding from the 1955 Declaration of the Supreme Soviet and convinced of the possibility of peaceful coexistence of all states, irrespective of their political and economic system, and also seeking to effect international co-operation in order to ensure world peace, they decided to form a Parliamentary Group of the U.S.S.R. and join the Inter-Parliamentary Union. The conference adopted the Statutes of the Parliamentary Group of the U.S.S.R. and elected a Provisional Bureau.

The conference urged all deputies of the Supreme Soviet to join the Group and instructed the Provisional Bureau to inform the Inter-Parliamentary Union about the formation of the Parliamentary Group of the U.S.S.R. and its desire to join the Inter-Parliamentary Union. The decision of the Conference was approved by the deputies and by the Soviet public. Within a month 93 per cent of the deputies of the Fourth Supreme Soviet joined the Parliamentary Group. On August 5, 1955, a general meeting of the Group was held attended by 891 deputies. It elected a Committee of the Parliamentary Group and decided to send a delegation to the 44th Conference of the Inter-Parliamentary Union (August 1955).

According to the Statutes of the Parliamentary Group, only deputies of the Supreme Soviet of the U.S.S.R. are elegible for membership. When they announce their desire to join the Group, they thereby approve the aims of the Inter-Parliamentary Union proclaimed in Article 1 of its Statutes. Each member pays dues to the amount of 1 ruble per month. The Group conducts annual meetings, usually concurrently with the Sessions of the Supreme Soviet. The general meeting is the supreme body of the Group. It guides its work and is authorised to pass decisions on any issues that may arise. In particular, it appoints representatives of the Group to Plenary Conferences and the Council Meetings and Standing Study Committees of the Inter-Parliamentary Union, hears the reports of delegates who have attended sittings of bodies of the Inter-Parliamentary Union, acquaints itself with the Conference and Council decisions, and makes representations to the Supreme Soviet of the U.S.S.R., its Presidium or the Council of Ministers of the U.S.S.R. on issues that require the decision of these organs. If the question is urgent, the Committee of the Group is authorised to make such a representation.

When a new Supreme Soviet is elected, during its first session or immediately after it, the general meeting of the Parliamentary Group of the U.S.S.R. is convened and it appoints the Committee of the Group. According to the new Statutes of the Parliamentary Group of the U.S.S.R., adopted by the general meeting of the group on August 3, 1966, the Committee consists of a chairman, two vice-chairmen, a secretary and 51 members.

The Committee conducts the affairs of the Group in the interim between its meetings and takes all necessary measures to achieve its purposes. It approves the plan of its activities, appoints, from among its own members, two representatives to the Council of the Inter-Parliamentary Union, usually its chairman or vice-chairman, or the secretary. The Committee also implements the decisions of the Conferences and the Council of the Inter-Parliamentary Union, conducts correspondence with the central organs of the Union, makes preparations for meetings of the Group, submits an annual report on the activities of the Group to the Bureau of the Inter-Parliamentary Union not later than March 31 each year, approves the budget of the Group and its accounts, forms sections of friendship with the corresponding bodies in other countries and approves their heads. The Committee is subordinate to the general meeting of the Group to which it reports on its activities. To conduct the Group's current business, the Committee elects a Bureau, which consists of a chairman, two vice-chairmen, a secretary and seven members. The Committee can make official announcements and statements both on its own behalf and on that of the Parliamentary Group of the U.S.S.R. in connection with international developments and on the affairs of the Inter-Parliamentary Union.

The Parliamentary Group of the U.S.S.R. publishes its own *Bulletin* (bi-yearly) which carries information about the activities of the Group and the Inter-Parliamentary Union, statements and appeals of the Group or its Committee to national parliamentary groups of other countries and to the Inter-Parliamentary Union, information on exchange of delegations, contacts and meetings with members of other parliaments, memoranda and draft resolutions of the Group submitted to the Inter-Parliamentary Union, records of the sittings of bodies of the Inter-Parliamentary Union and speeches made by Soviet delegates at these sittings, resolutions of the Conferences and decisions of the Council of the Inter-Parliamentary Union.

Of the 80 national parliamentary groups in the Inter-Parliamentary Union, the Parliamentary Group of the Soviet Union is the largest: at present it consists of 1,517 deputies of the Seventh Supreme Soviet of the U.S.S.R., including 767 deputies of the Soviet of the Union and 750 deputies of the Soviet of Nationalities. According to the present system of distribution of votes at the Inter-Parliamentary Union, the Parliamentary Group of the U.S.S.R. has the largest number of votes (22) and sends a delegation of 22 members to conferences.

The work of the Parliamentary Group of the U.S.S.R. and its Committee is conducted along three lines. These are:

1. Participation in the work of the Inter-Parliamentary Union;

2. Issue of statements and appeals on vital questions of international politics;

3. Exchange of delegations and visits by individual members of parliaments.

By joining the Inter-Parliamentary Union and taking part in its work, deputies of the Supreme Soviet of the U.S.S.R. have received additional opportunities to work for peace and promote the Leninist principles of peaceful coexistence in relations between countries with different social systems, and have been able to expand their contacts with members of other parliaments.

In pursuance of the principles underlying the peaceful foreign policy of the Soviet Union and seeking to bring about concerted action by members of all parliaments in defence of peace, the deputies of the Supreme Soviet of the U.S.S.R., both at sittings of various bodies of the Inter-Parliamentary Union and during other meetings with members of foreign parliaments, consistently strive for the relaxation of international tensions, general and complete disarmament, respect for the sovereignty of all states and non-interference in their domestic affairs, the abolition of colonialism in all its forms and manifestations and the expansion of economic, cultural and other contacts among nations. They use the rostrum of the Inter-Parliamentary Union to expose the schemes of imperialist forces that nurture plans of another war and launch aggressive actions.

Ever since the Parliamentary Group of the U.S.S.R. joined the Inter-Parliamentary Union, it has been active in all sittings of its bodies, including the annual Conferences (Helsinki, 1955; Bangkok,

1956; London, 1957; Rio de Janeiro, 1958; Warsaw, 1959; Tokyo, 1960; Brussels, 1961; Brasilia, 1962; Belgrade, 1963; Copenhagen, 1964; Ottawa, 1965; and Teheran, 1966).

It was largely due to the delegations of the Parliamentary Group of the U.S.S.R and other socialist countries that the leading bodies of the Inter-Parliamentary Union adopted decisions aimed at preserving peace and promoting international security. Their efforts also helped to stimulate confidence among nations and enhance the prestige of the Inter-Parliamentary Union in the world. For example, the Forty-Fourth Conference of the Inter-Parliamentary Union, the first attended by a delegation of the Parliamentary Group of the U.S.S.R., adopted a resolution on conditions for true peaceful coexistence between countries with different social and economic systems. This resolution declared that peaceful coexistence between states, irrespective of their economic and social systems, level of development, size and power, was in keeping with the aspirations of all peoples and their right to self-determination, and named the main principles to be observed, if trust and co-operation were to prevail among nations. The Conference believes, said the resolution, that to maintain peaceful coexistence and gradually effect international co-operation based on trust, the governments must loyally observe the provisions of international law, especially its principles:

a) mutual respect for territorial integrity, security and equality of every nation, unless it is a matter of aggression or colonial aggrandisement;

b) renouncement of all interference in the internal affairs of other countries;

c) renouncement of aggression;

d) renouncement of imperialism and racial discrimination.

The Conference proclaimed disarmament to be the basic condition for collective security and called on members of the Inter-Parliamentary Union to take all necessary measures for negotiating an agreement on disarmament. The Conference also urged broader international economic co-operation, regarding it as a major factor of peaceful coexistence.

The Forty-Fourth Conference expressed its solidarity with the Declaration of the Supreme Soviet of the U.S.S.R of February 9, 1955, which advocated direct contacts between parliaments of different countries in the interests of mutual understanding and preservation of peace, and appealed to all parliaments to take immediate steps in that direction.

The Soviet delegation to the Forty-Fourth Conference reported on its results to the Presidium of the Supreme Soviet of the U.S.S.R. and the general meeting of the Parliamentary Group. The general meeting expressed its satisfaction with the support given by the Forty-Fourth Conference to the principle of peaceful coexistence and its solidarity with the Supreme Soviet Declaration and noted that this Conference had made an important contribution to the cause of peace and security of nations.

On the initiative of the Parliamentary Group of the U.S.S.R. and with the support of delegations of other socialist countries and all progressive elements in the Inter-Parliamentary Union, other decisions aimed at promoting peace were adopted by the Union.

The Eightieth Session of the Union Council (1957) passed a special decision on the responsibility of members of parliament for averting war and stopping the arms race.

The Forty-Seventh Conference (1958) noted that urgent steps should be taken to lessen the danger of a new war and appealed to parliaments of all countries to work for the speediest possible convocation of a summit conference.

The Forty-Eighth Conference (1959) adopted the Soviet-sponsored resolution on banning war propaganda, which stated that war propaganda and any incitement to aggression were a danger to peace and that all governments ought to oppose such propaganda and incitement, and recommended legislation that would "forbid the use of literature, films, television, the press and toys encouraging violence and aggression".

The Forty-Ninth Conference (1960) condemned all manifestations of colonialism and racial discrimination, and also proposed that a world economic conference should be urgently held under the auspices of the United Nations.

The Fiftieth Conference (1961) expressed its deep concern over the deterioration of the international climate and the dangerous developments connected with the intensified arms race and appealed to the governments of the Great Powers to undertake serious negotiations on vital issues without any more delay and to work for their speedy solution in the interests of international security and peace.

The Fifty-First Conference of the Inter-Parliamentary Union was held in October 1962, in Brasilia, the new capital of Brazil. The moment was a very tense one due to the aggressive actions of the U.S. Government, which had enforced a sea blockade of the Republic of Cuba and brought the world to the brink of a thermo-nuclear war. The acute crisis provoked by the U.S.A. could not but affect the work of the Conference. The delegations of the Parliamentary Group of the U.S.S.R. and other socialist countries supported the Yugoslav draft resolution, which expressed concern at the sudden heightening of international tension caused by the blockade of Cuba, and demanded that the Conference should condemn the military actions of the U.S.A. Trying to justify the actions of their government the delegates of the United States blamed the crisis on the "intrigues of world communism". Their allegations that Cuba was a source of danger to the United States and the entire Western hemisphere were exploded by Soviet and other speakers.

The Fifty-Second Conference (1963) adopted the motion of the

Polish delegation supported by delegations of other socialist countries, which expressed approval for the Moscow Treaty Banning Nuclear Tests in the Atmosphere, Outer Space and Under Water and for the idea of atom-free zones in various regions of the world.

On December 14, 1960, the United Nations General Assembly, on the initiative of the Soviet Government, passed the Declaration on the Granting of Independence to the Colonial Countries and Peoples, which called for an immediate end to colonialism in all forms and manifestations.

The Parliamentary Group of the U.S.S.R. repeatedly brought up the question of the abolition of colonialism and submitted the corresponding memoranda and draft resolutions. The Fifty-Third Conference of the Union (1964) adopted a special resolution regarding the U.N. Declaration. The resolution, sponsored by the delegation of the parliamentary groups of the U.S.S.R. and other socialist countries, called upon the parliaments of all countries, especially those that possessed colonies, to press their governments in taking measures to implement the Declaration.

At the Inter-Parliamentary Union session in Dublin in April, 1965, the Soviet delegation, in accordance with the previously approved agenda, introduced memoranda and draft resolutions on the following questions: NATO multilateral forces, a danger to universal peace; a non-aggression pact between the NATO and Warsaw Treaty countries; reduction of war budgets; new prospects for international economic relations; the problem of apartheid in the light of the Universal Declaration of Human Rights and the U.N. Charter; the use of television and other mass media for instilling a spirit of peace and friendship in children and young people, etc. It should be noted that the majority of these questions were included in the programme of the Inter-Parliamentary Union for 1965.

Prompted by the desire to promote peace in Indo-China, the Parliamentary Group of the U.S.S.R. moved that the session in Dublin urgently discuss the question of U.S. aggression in Vietnam and submitted a draft resolution to the Council. In doing so it expressed the will of the Soviet people and their feelings of fraternal solidarity with the people of Vietnam, who were waging a heroic struggle against the American aggressors and their satellites, and the growing indignation of the peoples of the entire world with the aggressive actions of the U.S.A. in Vietnam. Vietnam was, essentially, the key political problem under discussion in Dublin. At the sittings of the Executive Committee and the Commision for Political Problems, International Security and Disarmament, which took place before the session of the Council, Soviet delegates and those of other socialist countries emphatically condemned the aggressive actions of the U.S.A. in Vietnam and demanded that the U.S.A. immediately discontinue its wanton bombings of the Democratic Republic of Vietnam and the use of poison gases and chemicals in South

Vietnam, that foreign troops be withdrawn, arms and strategic materials removed and the people of Vietnam given the opportunity to decide their own destiny.

In the course of the two-day debate at the sitting of the Council, representatives of the United States and their allies could produce no valid arguments against the facts cited by the delegates of the U.S.S.R. and other socialist countries, which gave indisputable proof of U.S. aggression. But the session in Dublin showed that members of the parliaments of some countries had not yet become fully aware of the danger entailed in the aggressive actions of U.S. imperialism and were not prepared to fight these actions vigorously enough. This largely accounted for the fact that the Council confined itself to a statement on the escalation of the war in Vietnam without naming the party responsible for this escalation.

By calling on all parties concerned "to begin negotiations without any preliminary conditions" the Council equated, as it were, the aggressor and his victim. It is obvious that negotiations conducted at gun-point, which is what the resolution of the Council virtually called for, would be a perversion of the legal concept of negotiations and could in no way help to put an end to aggression.

The Soviet delegation exploded the arguments of the representatives of the Parliamentary Groups of the U.S.A. and some other Western countries, who asserted that it would be contrary to the traditions of the Inter-Parliamentary Union to name the actual party responsible for the violation of peace. The Soviet delegates pointed out that the task of preserving and consolidating peace, which is a primary aim proclaimed in the Statutes of the Inter-Parliamentary Union, presupposes an active struggle against the concrete perpetrator of aggression, in this case the ruling circles of the United States. Since the draft resolution submitted by a group of delegates was unsatisfactory, and the amendments proposed by the delegation of the U.A.R. and Czechoslovakia were voted down, the delegates of the socialist countries and of some other countries voted against this resolution and seven delegations abstained.

At the Fifty-Fourth Conference of the Inter-Parliamentary Union that met in Ottawa in September 1965, the Parliamentary Group of the U.S.S.R. submitted a new draft resolution entitled "U.S. Aggression in Vietnam, a Serious Threat to World Peace and the Security of Nations".

Although the question of U.S. aggression in Vietnam was not officially included in the agenda, it was extensively discussed at the meetings of the Council and at plenary sessions of the Conference. In the course of heated debates the delegates of socialist and many other countries showed up the aggressive nature of the policy pursued by the U.S. ruling circles, who try to strangle the liberation struggle which keeps swelling despite their frantic efforts, and embraces ever new regions of the globe.

The criminal nature of the U.S. aggression was further exposed during the discussion of the Statement of the Supreme Soviet of the U.S.S.R. of December 9, 1965, on the U.S. aggression in Vietnam. On the initiative of the Parliamentary Group of the U.S.S.R. the session of the Union's Council, held in April 1966 in Australia, considered this Statement in which the Supreme Soviet of the U.S.S.R. condemned the armed intervention of the United States in South Vietnam and the aggression against the Democratic Republic of Vietnam, and called for efforts by the parliaments and governments of all countries to stop the U.S. aggression and give the Vietnamese people the opportunity to settle their internal affairs by themselves.

On the suggestion of the Parliamentary Group of the U.S.S.R., information about the Statement by the U.S.S.R. Supreme Soviet of August 3, 1966, on the escalation of U.S. aggression in Vietnam was included in the agenda of the Ninety-Ninth session of the Council, that took place in September 1966 in Teheran concurrently with the Fifty-Fifth Conference of the Union. The text of the Statement was previously sent out by the Bureau of the Union in Geneva to all the national member groups. The Soviet delegation declared that the U.S. criminal aggression against the Vietnamese people constituted a violation of the Geneva Agreements of 1954, the U.N. Charter and the universally accepted standards of international law. It aggravates international tensions and is a grave threat to international peace and security. The Soviet Union would continue doing all in its power to help the Vietnamese people drive out the U.S. invaders and liberate their country.

Chairman I. Spiridonov addressing the Soviet Parliamentary Group Committee on December 14, 1966

Thus, even before the Conference was opened, the Soviet delegation drew the attention of its participants and the press to the U.S. aggression in Vietnam. This question remained in the limelight throughout the work of the Conference.

The Parliamentary Group of the U.S.S.R. and those of other socialist countries repeatedly pointed out that peace in Europe and the world over was seriously endangered by the revival of militarism and revanchism in West Germany, by the efforts of West German ruling circles to represent all Germany, revise the results of the Second World War and obtain nuclear weapons, and by the plans for NATO multilateral nuclear forces that would give the West German militarists access to these weapons.

On May 17, 1967, the U.S.S.R. Parliamentary Group made a Statement on the military coup in Greece. It strongly condemned the repressions and arbitrary rule in Greece and called upon all the members of parliament, parliamentary groups of other countries and the Inter-Parliamentary Union to voice their protest against the anti-constitutional actions of the Greek ultra and to safeguard the principles of democracy and freedom.

The Soviet Parliamentary Group through its representatives on the Executive Committee, the Council and Standing Study Committees has been exercising considerable influence on the choice of issues taken up by the Inter-Parliamentary Union and the nature of the decisions adopted by that representative international organisation.

Like any other international body representing states with different social systems, the Inter-Parliamentary Union cannot but reflect the struggle between progressive and reactionary forces in the world.

Now that the Inter-Parliamentary Union has been joined by the parliamentary groups of socialist countries and countries recently liberated from colonial dependence, the prestige of this organisation has been greatly enhanced. Nonetheless, it does not yet play the role in international affairs that it is entitled to, considering that it unites parliamentarians who bear great responsibility and have considerable opportunity for promoting and consolidating peace.

Participation in the proceedings of the Inter-Parliamentary Union is the main, but not the only aspect of the work of the Parliamentary Group of the U.S.S.R.

Considerable importance is attached to the appeals and declarations made by the Parliamentary Group of the U.S.S.R. on various problems of international politics, as well as efforts to develop contacts with parliamentary groups of other countries through exchanges of delegations and visits by individual members of parliament, aimed at fostering mutual understanding and promoting peace and friendship among nations.

Along with other Soviet public bodies, the Parliamentary Group of the U.S.S.R. helped to set up the Soviet Committee for holding in Moscow a World Congress for General Disarmament and Peace. Its statement adopted in connection with this important event said that "the overwhelming majority of people shares the idea of peaceful coexistence of all states irrespective of their social system. But moral support for an idea, however broad, does not present a sufficiently powerful obstacle to the imperialists who are intent on unleashing another war. The key to peace lies in concerted action by all people of good will." The Soviet Members of Parliament have called upon parliamentary groups of other countries to work for the convocation of this congress.

More than two hundred members of parliament from different countries took part in the Congress. On June 13, 1962, they held a special meeting which published a communique that ran as follows: "Members of parliament must stimulate and mobilise public opinion in their respective countries in support of disarmament and peace. Being the people's representatives, they must use their parliaments for these purposes. They consider that war propaganda should be banned legislatively."

Participants in the meeting urged the dismantling of war bases and the withdrawal of troops from alien territory, the disbanding of military blocs and the discontinuance of interference in the internal affairs of other countries under any pretext whatsoever, the liberation of all colonies and the immediate conclusion of an agreement between the nuclear powers on the cessation of nuclear tests, general and complete disarmament under strict international control and the setting up of atom-free zones.

The Parliamentary Group of the U.S.S.R. actively responds to all international developments and works persistently in defence of justice, democracy and law. Among its actions along these lines were appeals on the armed intervention of the U.S.A. and Britain in the Lebanon and Jordan in the summer of 1958, the shooting of a demonstration in Leopoldville in January 1959, the murder of Patrice Lumumba, Prime Minister of the Republic of Congo (Leopoldville), and in defence of Antoine Gizenga, etc.

On March 2, 1965, the Committee of the Soviet Parliamentary Group made an appeal to parliamentary groups of all countries in connection with the intention expressed by the Government of the Federal Republic of Germany to discontinue, as from May 1965, the prosecution of nazi criminals on the ground that a considerable period had elapsed.

"The conscience of the peoples," the appeal said, "can never forgive the unleashing of the aggressive war and the monstrous crimes perpetrated by the nazi war criminals against peace and humanity such as tortures, the driving of people into slavery, mass murders of innocent civilians, brutal treatment of war prisoners, the barbarous destruction of thousands of towns and villages, and the tearing down of monuments of culture."

The Committee of the Soviet Parliamentary Group called on parliamentary groups of all countries to protest against the plans of the F.R.G. Government and to demand that nazi criminals should be made to answer for the crimes they had committed.

The Soviet delegation and those of other socialist countries vigorously supported the motion of the Polish delegation at the session of the Council in Dublin on "Non-Application of the Statute of Limitations to War Criminals and Crimes against Humanity". The motion was passed by an absolute majority with six abstentions, one of them being the delegate of the Federal Republic of Germany.

The Committee of the Soviet Parliamentary Group considered sympathetically the Declaration of the National Congress of the Dominican Republic of May 25, 1965, which condemned the flagrant interference of the U.S. Government in the internal affairs of that sovereign country. "By their armed intervention in the Dominican Republic," said the Statement by the Committee on June 3, 1965, "the circles that determine U.S. foreign policy have once again exposed themselves in the eyes of the world as the stranglers of national freedom and independence."

On December 9, 1965, the Committee of the Soviet Parliamentary Group adopted an appeal on the occasion of the twentieth anniversary of the Nuremberg trial of chief nazi war criminals. It pointed out that the verdict of the Nuremberg tribunal was the world's first condemnation of aggressive war as a crime against peace and humanity and a serious warning to all those who would prepare and launch aggression. The Committee called on all peace-loving forces to halt the West German revenge-seekers, prevent the arming of the Federal Republic of Germany with nuclear weapons, and strengthen world peace and security.

In its statement of December 14, 1966, on the occasion of the sixth anniversary of the National Liberation Front of South Vietnam, the Committee expressed its solidarity with the heroic Vietnamese people and wished it further successes in its sacred fight against U.S. aggression.

The Committee supported the policy of the Soviet Government in respect of Vietnam and pointed out that the stand taken by the Government of the Democratic Republic of Vietnam and the National Liberation Front of South Vietnam was in accord with the Geneva Agreements of 1954 and could serve as a reasonable basis for the settlement of the Vietnam issue.

The Parliamentary Group of the U.S.S.R. maintains broad contacts with parliamentary groups and individual members of parliament in other countries. Members of the Group have visited many countries and have had useful meetings with members of parliament in these countries. They delivered lectures and talks on general and specific political questions, helping to spread knowledge about the Soviet Union and its people.

In its turn the Soviet Union has played host to many members of foreign parliaments invited by the Soviet Parliamentary Group. The guests visit the various Soviet Republics and cities and are given every opportunity to acquaint themselves with the life and work of the Soviet people, the activities of the Supreme Soviet of the U.S.S.R. and of central and local legislative and administrative bodies.

Contacts between the Parliamentary Group of the U.S.S.R. and those of other socialist countries are particularly close.

The Soviet Parliamentary Group maintains ties with foreign members of parliament also through the following sections within it: Soviet-British, Soviet-Belgian, Soviet-Italian, Soviet-Mexican, Soviet-French and Soviet-Japanese. Corresponding sections exist in Britain, Belgium, Italy, France, Japan and Mexico. These sections exchange delegations and individual visits, as well as literature on the functioning of parliaments, and conduct meetings to discuss problems of mutual interest. Their activity undoubtedly promotes understanding and better relations between peoples.

SUPPLEMENT

National-Territorial Divisions and Population Distribution

	Date of formation	Population on January 1, 1967 ('000)	Territory ('000 sq. km.)
U.S.S.R.	December, 1922	234,396	22,402.2
R.S.F.S.R.	November, 1917	127,312	17,075.4

Including

Autonomous Republics

	Date of formation	Population on January 1, 1967 ('000)	Territory ('000 sq. km.)
1. Bashkirian	March, 1919	3,757	143.6
2. Buryat	May, 1923	780	351.3
3. Daghestan	January, 1921	1,361	50.3
4. Kabardinian-Balkar	December, 1936	530	12.5
5. Kalmyk	October, 1935	248	75.9
6. Karelian	July, 1923	707	172.4
7. Komi	December, 1936	974	415.9
8. Mari	December, 1936	653	23.2
9. Mordovian	December, 1934	1,014	26.2
10. North Ossetian	December, 1936	518	8.0
11. Tatar	May, 1920	3,127	68.0
12. Tuva	October, 1961	217	170.5
13. Udmurt	December, 1934	1,379	42.1
14. Checheno-Ingush	December, 1936	1,033	19.3
15. Chuvash	April, 1925	1,192	18.3
16. Yakut	April, 1922	646	3,103.2

Autonomous Regions

	Date of formation	Population on January 1, 1967 ('000)	Territory ('000 sq. km.)
1. Adygei	July, 1922	366	7.6
2. Gorno-Altai	June, 1922	169	92.6
3. Jewish	May, 1934	174	36.0
4. Karachai-Cherkess	April, 1928	330	14.1
5. Khakass	October, 1930	462	61.9

National Areas

	Date of formation	Population on January 1, 1967 ('000)	Territory ('000 sq. km.)
1. Agin-Buryat (Chita Region)	September, 1937	62	19.0
2. Komi-Permyak (Perm Region)	February, 1925	216	32.9
3. Koryak (Kamchatka Region)	December, 1930	37	301.5
4. Nenets (Arkhangelsk Region)	July, 1929	37	176.7
5. Taimyr, or Dolgano-Nenets (Krasnoyarsk Territory)	December, 1930	36	862.1
6. Ust-Orda Buryat (Irkutsk Region)	September, 1937	154	22.1

	Date of formation	Population on January 1, 1967 ('000)	Territory ('000 sq. km.)
7. Khanty-Mansy (Tyumen Region)	December, 1930	250	523.1
8. Chukotka (Magadan Region)	December, 1930	89	737.7
9. Evenki (Krasnoyarsk Territory)	December, 1930	12	767.6
10. Yamalo-Nenets (Tyumen Region)	December, 1930	73	750.3
Ukrainian S.S.R.	December, 1917	45,966	603.7
Byelorussian S.S.R.	January, 1919	8,744	207.6
Uzbek S.S.R.	October, 1924	10,896	449.6
including			
Kara-Kalpak A.S.S.R.	March, 1932	638	165.6
Kazakh S.S.R.	December, 1936	12,413	2,715.1
Georgian S.S.R.	February, 1921	4,611	69.7
including			
Abkhazian A.S.S.R.	March, 1921	471	8.6
Ajarian A.S.S.R.	June, 1921	301	3.0
South Ossetian Autonomous Region	April, 1922	102	3.9
Azerbaijan S.S.R.	April, 1920	4,802	86.6
including			
Nakhichevan A.S.S.R.	February, 1924	189	5.5
Nagorny Karabakh Autonomous Region	July, 1923	149	4.4
Lithuanian S.S.R.	July, 1940	3,026	65.2
Moldavian S.S.R.	August, 1940	3,425	33.7
Latvian S.S.R.	July, 1940	2,285	63.7
Kirghiz S.S.R.	December, 1936	2,749	198.5
Tajik S.S.R.	October, 1929	2,654	143.1
including			
Gorny Badakhshan Autonomous Region	January, 1925	93	63.7
Armenian S.S.R.	November, 1920	2,253	29.8
Turkmen S.S.R.	October, 1924	1,966	488.1
Estonian S.S.R.	July, 1940	1,294	45.1

Administrative Network on April 1, 1967

Union Republics	Autonomous Republics	Autonomous Regions	National Areas	Territories	Regions	Districts	City wards	Towns Total	of which: Republican, Territory, Regional, Area subordination	District subordination	Townships	Rural Soviets
R.S.F.S.R.	16	5	10	6	49	1,720	251	949	505	444	1,814	22,287
Ukrainian S.S.R.	—	—	—	—	25	475	85	381	113	268	821	8,544
Byelorussian S.S.R.	—	—	—	—	6	117	13	76	33	43	125	1,542
Uzbek S.S.R.	1	—	—	—	9	97	7	39	30	9	77	802
Kazakh S.S.R.	—	—	—	—	15	173	9	69	45	24	172	1,816
Georgian S.S.R.	2	1	—	—	—	67	7	48	11	37	54	909
Azerbaijan S.S.R.	1	1	—	—	—	60	9	51	9	42	119	912
Lithuanian S.S.R.	—	—	—	—	—	44	7	92	9	83	22	656
Moldavian S.S.R.	—	—	—	—	—	31	3	20	8	12	29	640
Latvian S.S.R.	—	—	—	—	—	26	5	56	7	49	33	546
Kirghiz S.S.R.	—	—	—	—	1	30	3	15	13	2	31	352
Tajik S.S.R.	—	1	—	—	—	37	3	18	12	6	38	273
Armenian S.S.R.	—	—	—	—	—	33	6	23	13	10	27	444
Turkmen S.S.R.	—	—	—	—	—	34	2	14	8	6	66	218
Estonian S.S.R.	—	—	—	—	—	45	3	33	6	27	24	237
Total	20	8	10	6	105	2,959	413	1,884	822	1,062	3,452	40,178

Representation in the Soviets: Central and Local

1. Percentage of Women and Non-Party People in the Soviets. Re-election of Deputies

Soviets	Total deputies	of whom		Not elected before
		women	non-Party people	
Supreme Soviet of the U.S.S.R. (1966)	1,517	425	376	1,015
per cent		28.0	24.8	66.9
Supreme Soviets of the Union Republics (1967)	5,830	1,962	1,837	3,968
per cent		33.7	31.5	68.1
Supreme Soviets of the Autonomous Republics (1967)	2,925	1,021	973	2,029
per cent		34.9	33.3	69.4
Local Soviets (1967)	2,045,418	875,302	1,100,531	1,010,903
per cent		42.8	53.8	49.4
including				
Territory, Regional and Area Soviets	25,747	10,826	10,766	14,953
per cent		42.0	41.8	58.1
District Soviets	223,220	95,319	100,946	130,530
per cent		42.7	45.2	58.5
Town Soviets	238,250	103,234	114,622	134,751
per cent		43.3	48.1	56.6
Ward Soviets	86,642	38,024	40,871	50,499
per cent		43.9	47.2	58.3
Rural Soviets	1,287,825	548,524	732,439	583,424
per cent		42.6	56.9	45.3
All types of Soviets	2,055,690	878,710	1,103,717	1,017,915
per cent		42.7	53.7	49.5

2. Education Statistics

Soviets	Total deputies	Education			
		primary	incomplete secondary	secondary	higher
Supreme Soviet of the U.S.S.R. (1966)	1,517	90	344	322	761
per cent		5.9	22.7	21.2	50.2
Supreme Soviets of the Union Republics (1967)	5,830	420	1,428	1,175	2,806
per cent		7.2	24.5	20.2	48.1
Supreme Soviets of the Autonomous Republics (1967)	2,925	255	691	499	1,480
per cent		8.7	23.6	17.1	50.6
Local Soviets (1967)	2,045,419	405,806	622,999	643,629	332,984
per cent		19.8	32.4	31.5	16.3
including					
Territory, Regional, Area Soviets	25,747	1,704	6,865	6,139	11,039
per cent		6.6	26.7	23.8	42.9
District Soviets	223,220	32,002	64,662	63,539	63,017
per cent		14.3	29.0	28.5	28.2
Town Soviets	238,250	16,872	71,124	83,314	66,940
per cent		7.1	29.8	35.0	28.1
Ward Soviets	86,642	2,403	24,872	30,201	29,166
per cent		2.8	28.7	34.8	33.7
Rural Soviets	1,287,825	327,005	434,169	390,384	136,267
per cent		25.4	33.7	30.3	6.7
Township Soviets	183,734	25,820	61,307	70,052	26,555
per cent		14.1	33.4	38.1	14.4
All types of Soviets	2,055,691	406,571	665,462	645,625	338,031
per cent		19.8	32.4	31.4	16.4

3. Occupation

	Total Deputies	Workers	Collective farmers	Managers, specialists and employees of enterprises and establishments	Workers in science, culture, art, education and health services	Workers of government bodies	Workers of Party, trade union, Y.C.L. bodies and other mass organisations	Other workers
Supreme Soviet of the U.S.S.R. (1966)	1,517	404	294	91	154	229	289	56
per cent		26.6	19.4	6.0	10.2	15.1	19.0	3.7
Supreme Soviets of the Union Republics (1967)	5,830	1,500	1,346	374	443	947	1,032	188
per cent		25.7	23.1	6.4	7.6	16.2	17.7	3.2
Supreme Soviets of the Autonomous Republics (1967)	2,925	700	561	286	233	525	563	57
per cent		23.9	19.2	9.8	8.0	17.9	20.8	2.0
Local Soviets (1967)	2,045,418	604,997	639,280	249,844	281,588	156,215	58,407	55,087
per cent		29.6	31.3	12.2	13.8	7.6	2.8	2.7
including								
Territory, Regional, Area Soviets	25,747	8,654	4,674	2,953	1,876	4,642	2,271	677
per cent		33.6	18.2	11.5	7.3	18.0	8.8	2.6
District Soviets	223,220	54,219	67,833	29,603	18,965	32,285	14,256	6,059
per cent		24.3	30.4	13.3	8.5	14.4	6.4	2.7
Town Soviets	238,250	112,902	3,437	53,233	31,037	15,789	11,273	10,579
per cent		47.4	1.4	22.3	13.0	6.6	4.7	4.5
Ward Soviets	86,642	41,965	46	19,457	11,777	5,241	5,064	3,092
per cent		48.4	0.1	22.5	13.6	6.0	5.8	3.6
Rural Soviets	1,287,825	305,837	552,186	105,004	189,849	88,285	21,988	24,676
per cent		23.7	42.9	18.2	14.7	6.9	1.6	1.9
Township Soviets	183,734	81,420	11,104	39,594	28,084	9,973	3,555	10,004
per cent		44.33	6.0	21.5	15.3	5.4	2.0	5.4
All types of Soviets	2,055,690	607,601	641,481	250,595	282,418	157,916	60,291	55,388
per cent		29.6	31.2	12.2	13.7	7.7	2.9	2.7

Standing Committees in Soviet Republics
on May 1, 1967

The Supreme Soviets of the Union and Autonomous Republics form the following standing committees: Credentials, Budgetary, Legislative Proposals. There are also Foreign Affairs Committees in some Union Republics. In addition the republican parliaments set up the following committees to handle the various branches of the economy and culture: industry, construction, transport and communications, agriculture, public amenities, public education and culture, public health and social security, trade and public catering, etc.

Standing Committees of the Supreme
Soviets of the Union Republics

Union Republics	Number of standing committees	Number of deputies elected to standing committees	Per cent of total number of deputies
R.S.F.S.R.	12	356	40.3
Ukrainian	17	281	81.2
Byelorussian	15	269	63.9
Uzbek	15	305	66.6
Kazakh	10	290	60.9
Georgian	14	310	77.7
Azerbaijan	10	240	63.2
Lithuanian	11	171	43.8
Moldavian	10	142	45.1
Latvian	11	185	59.7
Kirghiz	9	199	58.7
Tajik	15	253	80.3
Armenian	12	182	58.7
Turkmen	13	187	65.6
Estonian	10	140	78.7
Total	184	3,610	61.9

Standing Committees of the Supreme
Soviets of the Autonomous Republics

Autonomous Republics	Number of standing committees	Number of deputies elected to standing committees	Per cent of total number of deputies
Abkhazian	9	63	48.5
Ajarian	9	51	56.7
Bashkirian	11	193	78.1
Buryat	9	89	70.1
Daghestan	9	133	74.7
Kabardinian-Balkar	8	82	59.4
Kalmyk	9	81	70.4
Kara-Kalpak	13	119	72.6
Karelian	10	94	70.7
Komi	12	137	91.3
Mari	9	77	68.1
Mordovian	10	76	55.1
Nakhichevan	8	40	50.0
North Ossetian	9	79	61.7
Tatar	9	135	65.2
Tuva	8	84	76.4
Udmurt	11	133	74.7
Checheno-Ingush	10	88	59.1
Chuvash	10	107	71.8
Yakut	11	99	49.3
Total	194	1,960	67.0

Standing Committees of Local Soviets
Elected in March-April 1967

	Number of committees	Number of members of standing committees	Per cent of the total number of deputies of Soviets
Formed by :			
Territory, Regional and Area Soviets	1,662	22,073	85.7
District Soviets	25,930	187,688	84.1
Town Soviets	17,349	190,114	79.8
Ward Soviets	4,772	67,013	77.3
Rural Soviets	228,582	1,045,290	81.2
Township Soviets	23,505	154,335	84.0
Total	301,760	1,666,513	81.5

Name of standing committees	Number of committees	Number of commitee members	Per cent
Budgetary and Financial	47,832	242,958	14.6
Agriculture	43,467	251,525	15.1
Cultural and Educational	31,409	176,321	10.6
Public Education	21,429	135,782	8.1
Public Health and Social Security	18,144	120,115	7.2
Road Building and Town Planning	26,066	144,161	8.7
Industry, Construction, Transport and Communications	6,572	64,532	3.9
Trade and Public Catering	19,544	122,742	7.4
Public Amenities	2,895	25,672	1.5
Communal Services and Housing	5,614	53,059	3.2
Socialist Law	26,808	143,281	8.0
Credentials	48,779	160,927	9.6
Other committees	3,201	25,438	1.5
Total	301,760	1,666,513	100.0

REQUEST TO READERS

Progress Publishers would be glad to have your opinion of this book, its translation and design and any suggestions you may have for future publications.

Please send all your comments to 21, Zubovsky Boulevard, Moscow, U.S.S.R.